ACADEMIC ARMAGEDDON

About the Author

Mary Gallagher studied at UCD, Trinity College Dublin, the universities of Paris 7 and Paris 8 and at the École Normale Supérieure. She has been teaching French at UCD since 1991, but has also taught at Dundalk Institute of Technology, NUI Maynooth and several universities in France. She has acted as an external examiner for universities in Ireland, the UK and elsewhere in Europe and as a peer reviewer for US and Canadian academia. She has been a member of the Royal Irish Academy since 2005. Her previously published books include, along with several titles published in France, *Soundings in French Caribbean Writing since 1950: The Shock of Space and Time* (Oxford University Press, 2002) and *World Writing: Poetics, Ethics, Globalization* (University of Toronto Press, 2008).

ACADEMIC ARMAGEDDON

An Irish Requiem for Higher Education

Mary Gallagher

The Liffey Press

Published by
The Liffey Press Ltd
Raheny Shopping Centre, Second Floor
Raheny, Dublin 5, Ireland
www.theliffeypress.com

A catalogue record of this book is
available from the British Library.

ISBN 978-1-908308-05-4

Printed in Ireland by Sprint Print.

Contents

Contents

Author's Note

This book tries to make sense of the growing disorientation of Higher Education worldwide. Its central focus, however, is on Ireland. Although I stand over the apocalyptic title, I do appreciate that every battle has an afterwards. Furthermore, there are always green zones. Apologies are due therefore to those whose efforts to fight the good fight for Higher Education have been omitted, misrepresented or otherwise disrespected.

I am grateful to David Givens for publishing this book. I am also indebted to the many present and former colleagues and students whose sense of humour and feel for what matters have made – and still make – a big difference. I only refrain from thanking them by name for fear of implying that they share all of my views. They know who they are and how much this book owes to them.

For Emmanuelle and her brothers and sister

1

From the Groves of Academe to the Corporate Campus

With public discourse on Irish Higher Education lurching from one call for radical reform to the next, something is clearly amiss. In fact, Higher Education worldwide appears to be in crisis. And although that crisis is global and systemic, it is often projected in Ireland onto one isolated feature of the Irish second- or third-level education system specifically: the Leaving Certificate; the points system; private secondary schools; grind schools; the allegedly inflated remuneration of teachers, lecturers or university presidents; not enough college class-time; too many universities; not enough universities; too much rote learning; inadequate exchequer funding for research or capital investment; rising tuition fees. Each of the above has been targeted as the principal problem, which, if solved, would give Ireland the Higher Education system it wants and needs. But what sort of system would that be? For most pundits, the answer seems obvious. Just as the 'top' Irish secondary schools appear to be those identified in *The Irish Times* league tables as those whose students proceed in greatest numbers to the top-points university courses, proponents of Irish educational reform want what the US and the UK have, that is, systems boasting the highest numbers of globally-rated 'top' universities. Of the many questions raised by this reflex response, two immediately come to mind. First, why have the problems besetting the US Higher Education system played such a starring role in all of President Obama's State of the Union addresses? And why would Ireland want or need a third-level system in which top-layer colleges charge, as they do in the UK and US, tuition fees of five digits, the first of which is rarely a one in the US?

So is something going wrong with Higher Education? If so, what? And where does Ireland sit in that picture? And why does it matter enough to write – or read – a whole book about it?

THE REAL UNIVERSITY?

A recent literary verdict on these questions appears in a novel by J.M. Coetzee, one of the most distinctive voices of contemporary writing and laureate of the 2003 Nobel Prize for Literature. According to the narrator of his *Diary of a Bad Year* (2008), the university's number is up.

> In the days when Poland was under Communist rule, there were dissidents who conducted night classes in their homes, running seminars on writers and philosophers excluded from the official canon (for example, Plato). No money changed hands, though there may have been other forms of payment. If the spirit of the university is to survive, something along those lines may have to come into being in countries where tertiary education has been wholly subordinated to business principles. In other words, the real university may have to move into people's homes and grant degrees for which the sole backing will be the names of the scholars who sign the certificates.

Coetzee's claim is not that Higher Education is bound for oblivion. It is rather that intrinsic educational values are no longer driving universities. And that, in so far as these values are essential to the survival of Higher Education, they will have to be put on life-support, either inside or outside the current university wasteland. This vision may seem fanciful. However, it is only slightly less pessimistic than the one put forward by such authorities as former Harvard presidents. Furthermore, when dire predictions of the demise of academia find their way out of specialist writing and into world literature, there is a strong possibility that there really is something important going on. For Coetzee, real Higher Education is just as surely throttled by the unrestrained rule of the market as by absolutist state control. If this is so, it means that, just when academia has become a major global industry, flourishing as never before, it may actually be in trouble. As we will see throughout this book, many well-positioned sources seem to agree that the commercial distention of Higher Education is indeed another of our epoch's bubbles. For them, the Higher Education business, though 'too big to burst', and though it is benign in comparison to some of history's more toxic hoaxes, is hollow to its core.

It would be easy to dismiss such observations as motivated by a naïve anti-business, anti-market, anti-commercial, anti-industrial, anti-management bias. Yet this is not so. It is surely obvious to all that the innovation, commerce and industry which kept the 'West' to the fore for centuries are going to have to keep all humanity afloat for the foreseeable future. And part of the point of Higher Education (though not its entire purpose) is surely to facilitate that buoyancy. But how is Higher Education to support humanity's economic and technological endeavour in the way they deserve to be supported? That is, with a 'highly' educated population, a population able, for example, to recognise unrestrained financial speculation as a perversion of economics. How indeed, if not by turning out thinking graduates who

3

understand their subjects in sufficient depth and detail to be regarded as truly qualified and educated people. To achieve this end, however, education has to be true first and foremost, and across the board, to educational standards and values and *not* to the imperatives and principles of business. Respecting and supporting business and industry is one thing; turning education itself into an industry or a business is another thing altogether, and in fact any such shift will probably work ultimately against the interests of bona fide industries and real businesses.

THE FAKE UNIVERSITY

The purpose of this first section of *Academic Armageddon* is to give a bird's eye view of the contemporary academic battleground. The following two sections explore the trenches in greater detail. Section Two tries to explain the US and UK experience, and Section Three looks at the Irish context more specifically.

J.M. Coetzee suggests that the contemporary university is not a 'real university' because it has been overrun by business principles. The argument would go like this: businesses commercialise goods or services in order to generate profit; Higher Education, on the other hand, aims to generate not just well-trained professionals but also enlightened and informed citizens, and therefore constitutes a public good. The USA offers a very clear example of a society that has consistently glorified free enterprise. It also offers, as we will see, a cautionary example of how difficult it is to rein in markets that have been allowed to run amok in realms that should never have been subordinated to unrestrained commercial interests in the first place. Nobody could quarrel with the idea of running Higher Education sustainably, without waste or extravagance. However, marketing it as a saleable product or a 'brand' risks turning it into something else, something that is neither true nor thought-ful. We will see that marketing and speculation are playing an increasingly important role in Higher Education in those parts of the world most deeply plugged into the global nexus. And the problem with speculating on education is not dissimilar to, though perhaps just as serious as, the problem with the wild financial and property speculation with which Ireland recently became too well acquainted. It's the problem of distinguishing between ends and means, and of keeping a sense of direction and value. As early as the mid-nineties, a North American academic, Bill Readings, admitted to beginning many of his sentences with the phrase, 'In a real University . . .' (in *The University in Ruins*, 1996). For Readings, the contemporary university is not just a fiction that falls short of an 'ideal' authenticity. It is actually in ruins, wrecked by its subordination to the 'generalised rule of the cash-nexus'.

By and large, Irish public discourse on Higher Education has not taken account of the intense debates that have been raging about this problem in other places. This parochial approach is, in itself, problematic. It is bad enough to be in a vortex, but surely worse to be ignorant of the scale of the spin. That is why this book tries to look beyond Ireland, taking soundings elsewhere of what seems to be a very similar scenario of disorientation to the one currently simmering within Irish Higher Education. So what exactly is wrong with the Higher Education model that has been in the ascendant globally over the past two decades, and that has been belatedly but catastrophically adopted in some quarters in Ireland too? And who cares?

CORPORATE RENDITION

On the first question, J.M. Coetzee's diagnosis of business creep seems accurate enough. But how does this subordination of Higher Education to commercial ends manifest itself as a perversion of education? This question can be answered to some extent by pointing to the abuse of language within and around Higher Education. Broadly speaking, the language of advertising and public relations has infiltrated academia. This would not matter so much if Higher Education were simply a frilly 'finishing school' for the planet's privileged youth, or if it were a mere formality, an automatic ticket-booth for the journey to prosperity. But surely, as part of the educational continuum, Higher education aspires above all to provide a reliably safe haven for a truthful thoughtfulness. If 'Higher' education, or any part of it, is neither 'higher' nor focused on real enlightenment, then its legitimacy and credibility are at risk. The light of education is not the harsh neon of advertising. It does not violate the nutritious shade of uncertainty or contradiction. Indeed, the higher it aims, the more education courts the shadows which soften the hard, definitive lines of knowledge, keeping them forever open to further probing. Real educators know that the penumbra of uncertainty is not to be feared. What is dangerous, rather, is the blank – and often thoughtless – certainty of flood-lighting.

So what does it mean when language is abused to cover up what is really going on in academia? What happens when the work of Higher Education is captured by marketing propaganda? Propaganda is as old as warfare and it is interesting that today's military operations are sometimes disguised as educational or development projects. Witness the activities of Bancroft Global Development [sic], a private US security firm founded in 1999 by a Princeton graduate whose website – before it was essentially shut down – presented the mission of this 'charitable' organisation as taking violence out of public discourse. Originally listed as a charity centred on making safe unexploded ordnance, Bancroft is still a not-for-profit and therefore tax-exempt company. Yet as such it is one of the major private security firms profiting from the perfect storm that is Somalia. It has been providing, for example, expert training and frontline 'mentoring' support to the African Union counter-insurgency forces operating around Mogadishu. Its mercenary-led training services there have been widely praised as helpful (diminishing, for example, civilian casualties by teaching smarter sniping), but they are also highly lucrative. According to an undenied 2011 article in the *New York*

Times, the bill is settled by the Ugandan and Burundi governments, whom the US then reimburses.

The Bancroft example illustrates perfectly the rationale of 'plausible deniability' which increasingly governs the public realms – defence, healthcare, education, security – in our predominantly corporate age. This rationale is of a piece with the relentless sub-contracting, out-sourcing and privatisation of professional expertise – military or academic, for example. And it is usually framed in supra-national or 'global' terms – 'global development' in the case of Bancroft for example – rather than in terms of specific national or named interests. And as such, its ethos is arguably as fundamentally non-democratic as it is evasive.

So what kind of 'global development' is 'Higher Education' really and truly enabling today? And what is 'higher' about 'education' systems which seem to be producing, in places at least, an obvious subsidence of the most basic academic standards? What kind of faith can we place in language when institutions entrusted with the frontline defence of 'critical thinking' are subverted by off-the-peg 'group-guff'? Or indeed when the very notion of academic freedom is cancelled by requiring academics to serve not universal values but rather a specific 'corporate apparat'? What happens when the 'quality' or 'excellence' of an academic unit is described and measured primarily or exclusively in relation to its compliance with commercially strategic imperatives? How long until language and thought give way under the strain?

How can Higher Education retain its aspiration to human elevation, or at very least to uprightness, if it actually underwrites untruth? And isn't the self-contradictory combination of grade inflation and falling academic standards as much an untruth as any systemic displacement of real educational value by commercial proxies: extortionate tuition fees, off-scale salaries or bonuses for academic managers, etc? Wherever the principal, or the only, uplifts associated with Higher Education are its elevated price-tag and ever more implausibly inflated grade outcomes there is clearly a problem with the basic legitimacy of an entire system. Moreover, this problem is viral: once it attacks the moral and intellectual fibre of the educational organism, it cannot easily be contained. For example, Irish universities may now be complaining about the fact that they are enrolling ever more students groomed by grinds or grind-schools, and fed a staple diet of exam-focused revision and sample-exam books. Yet surely the academic standards of third-level education in Ireland as elsewhere have been, of necessity, voraciously adjusting to this malnourished student intake over more than a decade by substituting quantum for quality, with entirely predictable consequences. Similarly, any university – or part of a university – anywhere that enrols quotas of overseas students charged up to eighteen times the annual tuition fees paid by domestic students must surely expect such extortionate profiteering to propagate commoditisation (and worse) right throughout the system.

TROUBLE ABROAD AND BRINGING IT ALL BACK HOME

Following the popping of the property bubble and the near collapse of the banking system, levels of trust in Irish institutions are not high. From financial institutions to the Catholic Church, from the state training agency (Fás) to the health service, from politics to trade unions to education, all have been subject to a steep drop in perceived credibility. Although some parts of the Higher Education system have been leaking trust too, on the whole the sector is held up as the single great hope for the future: it is waved from most political flag-posts as the main avenue to the 'knowledge economy' that is going to save the nation. No doubt in some respects this is a legitimate hope and many individuals and many groups are strenuously trying to realise it against the odds. In other respects, though, it seems to be based on a failure to confront the prevailing global view of Higher Education as the sale and purchase of intellectual property, that is, as a lucrative subset of High Capitalism (with its privatised rewards, but socialised costs and risks).

Many of the woes afflicting Higher Education have been caused by the collapse of respect for two important distinctions. First of all, between intrinsic and exchange values; and secondly, between critical and uncritical thinking, or between thinking and its opposite. That collapse is not unique to the Irish system and can be traced back at least as far as the English-speaking trade-winds of globalisation. These global gales gusted into Irish colleges and universities from across the Atlantic – perhaps after a little managerialist detour round the UK.

To recognise that the post-millennium 're-structuring' of Ireland's Higher Education system was essentially imitative of two key international, 'Anglo' models – North American and UK/ Australian – is to acknowledge that the damage inflicted since about 2004 upon Irish Higher Education was not invented by some uniquely malign Irish ingenuity. However, if some of Ireland's Higher Education institutions only really began in 2004 to 'play catch up', as one university president put it at the time, this does raise some questions. If it was a case of rousing so-called Sleeping Giants to their 'manifest destiny' as Galloping Goliaths, what sort of due diligence was done on what well-placed international sources were already viewing in the nineties as a race to perdition? How could it be that (some) Irish universities would fall, so very late in the day, for such an extreme version of the very formulae and systems that had been causing – at point of origin – such intractable problems over time?

With the two notable exceptions of 'world league' envy and the imperative of global growth via increased international recruitment, the real threats to Higher Education are rarely, if ever, discussed in public in Ireland. Indeed, public debate is at such a low level that the global rankings race and internationalisation are usually presented as panaceas rather than as risks or threats. Higher Education is of course by no means the only area suffering from this contraction of debate and shortening of vision. The grip of transnational markets has indeed tightened to such a degree that, right across the world, people's entire economic and social future now seems to be in the power of feral commercial forces that few can claim to understand or track comprehensively, let alone forecast, influence or counteract. There may be countries, although no perfect example comes to mind (France perhaps? well, maybe Norway?), which might be more self-sufficient or self-confident culturally than Ireland, and which might therefore have succumbed either less rapidly or less completely to the neoliberal mirage propagated from within the Anglo world of credit ratings. Most, though, seem tempted to surrender their Higher Education systems to a greater or lesser extent and against more or less resistance to the faceless tyranny of global markets. The Irish sell-out has been particularly stark and unresisted, in spots at least, so that the main question now is just how much more of the collective soul Ireland's colleges are still prepared to hand over. In making that decision, one point is important to bear in mind. As the US experience shows, just as the balance of an entire economy could be undone by confidence tricks like subprimes, so too entire education systems are destabilised by rampant commoditisation and aggressive speculation on educational products. Some universities (Yale, Harvard, MIT, Oxbridge) may 'get away' with playing the global markets while continuing to provide superlatively safe havens for intrinsic academic values and standards. As we will see, though, not all the academic staff – nor even all the leaders – of these Higher Education stars are convinced that speculation is the way to go. Thus, while individual universities – the above-named, for example, or indeed the great public universities of London or California – may still appear to stand securely on the internationally enviable academic reputation that they helped to earn over decades for Higher Education in the UK and US, it is surely important to ask why some vocal insiders from within those two systems are voicing such urgent concerns about the integrity of Anglo-American Higher Education as a whole.

US Higher Education: A Global Model?

Over the past five decades at least, the US has functioned as an academic magnet. In most fields, the combined creative and critical resonance of its investment of unparalleled resources in academic endeavour has been incalculable. Perhaps that is why few could have predicted the unfurling in recent years of a tidal wave of insider jeremiads, not just journal articles but also full-length books, all focussing on the compromised state of contemporary US academia in general, particularly but not exclusively in the humanities. The authors of this material, mostly ostensibly 'successful' academics with no obvious axe to grind, and in some cases with more to lose than to gain, are claiming that the business model driving American Higher Education has turned out to be toxic for certain core academic standards and principles over the system as a whole.

One of these authors is Cary Nelson, for five years President of the American Association of University Professors (AAUP). Nelson's view lends credibility to the scenario imagined in Coetzee's novel. 'Within a very few years, higher education as we have known it may largely cease to exist,' he writes in *Office Hours: Activism and Change in the Academy* (2004), a book co-written with Stephen Watt. For these two authors:

> Higher education as we have known it for nearly half a century is in the process of unravelling. Few of the forces shaping its future are easy to welcome. Most will be destructive, especially to the most professionally vulnerable employees and the most financially vulnerable arts and humanities disciplines.

In an earlier collaborative effort, *Academic Keywords: A Devil's Dictionary for Higher Education* (1998), Nelson and Watt had already issued a clear warning to this effect:

> Higher education is in genuine trouble. There is no conspiracy to uncover, but there are multiple, uncoordinated forces working to alter higher education for the worse, not the better.

As we will see further on, the collapse of many, if not most, of the core principles of Higher Education across today's world does indeed appear to be the unintended consequence of several colliding factors. *Office Hours* identifies these as 'economic, demographic and political' in nature, but it also mentions the loss of 'intellectual independence and institutional influence' of academics. This last point begs a question. If academics are not in charge of Higher Education anymore, then who is? And if this change in the steering structure is linked to the 'unravelling' of Higher Education as we have known it 'for nearly half a century', then how has this happened and what are the consequences for the public interest? The answer to this question is spelled out in some detail by Nelson in *Academic Keywords*, especially in an essay entitled 'The Corporate University'. This piece has not dated and is probably unsurpassed in its insights into the academy's capitulation to commercial pressures.

Another source of worrying prognoses is Derek Bok, former president of Harvard University. In fact, Bok was twice made president of Harvard and the world's number one university named its Research Centre on Teaching and Learning after him. On the second occasion Bok was recalled *in extremis* from retirement in order to replace Larry Summers, a former President of the World Bank, who had resigned shortly after he lost two votes of confidence when Harvard academic staff in the Humanities objected to various aspects of his management style. Bok is the author of *Universities in the Marketplace: The Commercialisation of Higher Education* (2003). He argues as follows:

> [T]o keep profit-seeking within reasonable bounds, a university must have a clear sense of the values needed to pursue its goals with a high degree of quality and integrity. When the values become blurred and begin to lose their hold, the urge to make money quickly spreads throughout the institution.

Although fairly unambiguous in his warning about the direction being taken by Higher Education, Bok was criticised by some academics for pulling his punches. For example, in his review in the *New York Times* (May 2003), the newly appointed president of Amherst College, Anthony W. Marx, stated that Bok's diagnosis did not go far enough. Marx's review of Bok's book is tellingly entitled 'Academia for Sale (Standards Included)' and in it the Amherst President is very frank:

> On campus, efforts to attract and retain satisfied student 'consumers' feed grade inflation and the dumbing down of courses.

It is worth quoting one further example of the pessimism of USA academic analysts. In her recent study, *The Lost Soul of Higher Education: Corporatisation, the Assault on Academic Freedom and the End of the American University* (2010), Ellen Schrecker analyses the contemporary threat to the core function of US universities. For this historian – well known for her work on the ravages caused by the McCarthyist witch-hunts in US academia – the main purpose of American universities is again today in 'serious danger'. This time, the threat is what she calls 'corporate-style restructuring'. Schrecker does not mince her words. For her, corporate re-engineering is proving so toxic that unless US academics organise, academic freedom may well disappear from their campuses and the 'academic profession as we know it could vanish from the face of the earth'.

> The academy has always had to fend off external challenges from politicians and others who want to eliminate unpopular professors or censor the curriculum. Those pressures have not abated. But now the nation's colleges and universities are also confronting demands for so-called reforms that would substitute economic considerations of productivity and cost-effectiveness for the traditional educational values of enlightenment and individual growth. In the name of efficiency and accountability, groups and individuals both on and off the campus threaten to transform higher education into a source of vocational training and corporate research. In the process, the nation's faculties [academics] have been shunted aside.

Two points need to be underlined here. First of all, wherever this sorry tale has unfolded, and it is already an exhaustingly familiar saga in some Irish Higher Education scorch-spots, the principal losers have not been tenured academics. In fact, securely employed academics have little to gain – for themselves, at least – by facing down Armageddon. The principal casualty is rather the ideal of Higher Education as a public good, more specifically, the ability of academics, tenured or not, to serve and protect that ideal, less for themselves than for their students, the wider society and posterity.

Secondly, Schrecker's identification of the traditional values of Higher Education as being 'enlightenment' and 'individual growth' needs some qualifying comment. The problem is that, historically, institutions of Higher Education have not always, not automatically, been on the side of the angels. In other words, the academic pursuit of knowledge did not inoculate Europe (the continent that was the chief avowed champion of 'Enlightenment') against a willingness to practice whole-scale human exploitation, oppression, enslavement, ethnocide and even genocide. If the Shoah is the ultimate reference here, Western imperialism and the bloody wars of colonisation and decolonisation amply demonstrate that a highly developed academic culture is not automatically protective against the virus of barbarity. Similarly, the take-off of the global 'knowledge economy' hasn't stopped both private and public industry in France, the UK, the US, Russia, Pakistan, China, Iran, North Korea etc. from pouring hundreds of billions of dollars annually *not* into real human and planetary development but into weapons of mass destruction. Mightn't the aspirations of Higher Education be best represented, therefore, by an ever-questioning, ever-vigilant approach to the values of 'knowledge' and 'enlightenment', one that remembers that 'light' can be used as much to blind us as to allow us to see? And mightn't those aspirations be better served by a less uncritical, expansionist or acquisitive notion of human flourishing than 'growth', whether collective or individual?

Notwithstanding these caveats, Schrecker's indictment of 'the structural changes that have transformed the very nature of American higher education' is highly relevant for Ireland now, even if it is difficult to compare the Irish Higher Education system with that of the US or even with that of the UK. After all, the entire Higher Education sector of Ireland is smaller in scale than one large state university in the US. Indeed, the College of Arts and Science of the University of Arizona alone has about as many students – in excess of 20,000 - as the total student head-count of Ireland's largest university, UCD. And yet, it is also difficult to see how, if Ireland follows the example of Higher Education in the US, or even the UK, it will not also reproduce the flaws currently being complained of within those systems. These include:

- The erosion of academic experience as a developmental and transformative public good, and its replacement by the credentialism that treats education as a commercial or business transaction

- The promotion of a corporate culture of conformity which undermines independent, critical and creative thinking

- The counterproductive managerialist stranglehold both on academic work and on fully transparent and participative university governance.

WHAT'S WRONG WITH GROWING THE GLOBAL BUSINESS OF HIGHER EDUCATION?

It seems that the so-called 'developed' world has entered a 'post-industrial' and maybe even a 'post-democratic' phase which goes under the name of 'globalisation'. It also seems that no viable alternative to the empire of transnational financial capitalism is forthcoming. Instead of squaring up to that fact, instead of trying to imagine a universally equitable human future beyond what the (putatively) global market has been able to deliver up until now, Western Higher Education has been busy applying the old industrial logic of output maximisation and utilitarianism. Yet, in a world where unemployment and redundancy are likely to rise rather than diminish – certainly in the immediate term, probably periodically and perhaps even continually – people surely need education for living at least as much as for buying and selling; at least as much for leading curious, questioning, free, whole, thoughtful, just and humane lives as socially responsible, resourceful planetary citizens with developed inner lives, as for making and spending money (sustainably) for themselves or for Ireland. It's not either/or, of course, but in practice the two imperatives can pull away from each other.

From Harvard to the National University of Ireland, from the University of Singapore to the Sorbonne, corporate universities have been absorbed into the globalisation agenda of hyper-capitalism. When Drew Faust, the historian who is currently President of Harvard (the university consistently ranked top, or near top, in the world), gave a talk at the Royal Irish Academy in Dublin in 2010, the principal 'good news' of her lecture was that the number of universities world-wide was growing and that access to universities including Harvard itself, or at least Harvard outreach, was also growing. The trouble with this view is that growth is not necessarily and automatically good. Nature makes this point quite clearly: contagion and metastasis can be just as dangerous as failure to grow. Integrity, justice or education might be absolute values, but growth or spread are not. In fact, Harvard – despite the fact that it has been topping the league of the greatest universities in the world – is not entirely immune from the global loss of educational direction. We could see it in fact as a conflicted corporate person. In this sense, its on/off love affair with its former president, Larry Summers, long-time champion of market deregulation and consultant to many of the top US hedge funds, is no less emblematic of that disorientation than the sceptical soul-searching of Derek Bok, already mentioned as the former Harvard President who came back from retirement to step into Summers's abruptly abandoned shoes.

As President of Harvard, Summers showed a colourful disregard for political correctness by opining on taboos as diverse as women's intelligence relative to men's and the academic seriousness of African American studies. As chief economist of the World Bank, he signed a memo that made jokingly approving reference to the practice of toxic dumping in Africa. Yet, despite these controversies and despite his track record of support for economic policies largely favourable to financial kleptocracies, Summers was appointed by Barack Obama in 2009 as President of the National Economic Council, a position he held for just about two years before returning to Harvard as head of an academic think-tank, the Centre of Business and Government at the university's Kennedy School of Government. What the resilience of Summers's career chiefly shows is the difficulty, experienced both by political regimes and by intellectual institutions, of breaking definitively with certain failed ideologies. Both his political and his academic afterlives testify to the almost inexplicable persistence of a cloud of plausibility around the neo-liberal, neo-con value-system that, although it is thoroughly discredited, has yet to be properly replaced.

Is Higher Education's global growth agenda all about the development of a deeper global commitment to a universal educational ideal? Or is it overly concerned with growing the global market for the corporate university? In other words, what exactly does it mean when University College London calls itself London's 'Global University', or when UCD entitles its strategic plan 'Forming Global Minds'? It would seem that the obligatory term 'global' in university straplines refers principally, if not exclusively, to the overseas market for Higher Education. Isn't it just code for overseas market share? If so, then instead of referring to an inclusive ideal of 'no mind left behind' on the journey to universal human enlightenment, the current global aspirations of Higher Education are focussed principally on market penetration and on branding and pricing. And as such they have more to do with image than with substance. Hence, whenever Higher Education shows its corporate or commercial hand – and nowhere is this self-betrayal as dramatic as in exorbitant tuition fees or excessive executive remuneration – the trouble is not just the profiteering itself, but the prevailing silence about the implications. Above all, the corporate rendition of Higher Education reveals a heartbreaking emptiness at the very core of the whole educational enterprise, both at home and abroad.

Corporate universities with a brand to develop overseas typically join 'global' networks or syndicates like Universitas 21. Indeed, Ireland's UCD belongs to this grouping, which also includes Hong Kong University, the University of Virginia and the National University of Singapore. Other more prestigious associations include the US Ivy League and the UK Russell group, to which both University College London and Queen's University Belfast belong. It goes without saying that 'unbranded' universities need not apply to these clubs for rising corporate players. In other words, the global league does not include struggling institutions like the University of Tehran or Birzeit University in Palestine, vast open institutions such as the Autonomous University of Mexico, or those with seven-digit student enrolment numbers like Indira Gandhi National Open University in India.

The corporate university's fixation on growing its global market has prompted some Yale academics to criticise their university's 2011 establishment in Singapore of its first joint campus overseas (with the National University of Singapore). Yale academics like Christopher Miller have argued in the *Higher Education Chronicle* that Yale is 'following the money' with no regard for the effect of its strategy on standards of academic or intellectual freedom. They believe that if educational development was really its priority, Yale would have established its overseas campus elsewhere. It might, for example, have looked towards India, towards Central or South America, or Africa or even Europe.

Of course, there is always a possibility that Yale hopes that its venture will turn the shared Singapore campus, and perhaps even Singapore itself, into a haven of (academic) freedom. And maybe the plethora of mostly US-based private security firms scrambling for Somalia-based contracts are, as one of them – Bancroft – claims, genuinely promoting the cause of 'global development'. For one of the most respected living philosophers of ethics, however, it is extremely difficult to reconcile social justice with market rule. In his most recent book, *God, Philosophy, Universities* (2009), Alisdair MacIntyre gives a scathing definition of contemporary universities:

> . . . wonderfully successful business corporations subsidised by tax exemptions and exhibiting all the acquisitive ambitions of such corporations.

The corporatisation of Higher Education throws up many ethical, political and educational problems in addition to the more prosaic economic question of long-term sustainability. As

Higher Education's 'think-tank' energies are absorbed in chasing money, no one has yet explained how the brash magic of global branding will play out in the longer term. What will enable once-reputable universities to recover the legitimacy lost by associating themselves with organisations that have been flogging their brands, syndicated or not, by selling – for example – over-priced medical training and drug development on the global market? Perhaps individual figureheads are protected by a sort of 'plausible deniability' which enables them to plead ignorance of 'unintended consequences'. Yet, as these individuals hop with apparent immunity and impunity from one institutional platform to the next, the whole academic ecosystem is being irreversibly damaged by the blowback from the destruction of academic priorities. In other words, the destruction of the very priorities that established certain academic 'brands' in the first place.

Unlike some German, Japanese, Spanish, South American, Italian, Indian, Scandinavian or even French universities (as yet, anyway), the corporate university – genetically Anglo – is relentlessly and 'globally' competitive in ambition. In concrete terms, the brand of corporate universities depends, in an entirely circular manner, on the academic attainment and promise of the students seeking to enrol. Ultimately, only high demand from the most academically qualified students who can effectively go anywhere they want will keep a university's 'brand' over time up there with the best. For now, however, university league tables give credit to universities for the numbers of international students enrolled as though raw quantum were proof of anything. Meanwhile, well-endowed US universities vie with one another in offering scholarship packages to the most academically able of international graduate students, while less endowed institutions (such as Irish universities), including those whose targets for international students are as high as 30 per cent of the student population, count on these students as income streams. Furthermore, many outsource their overseas marketing and recruitment operations to external agents. But what is the likelihood of those 'global' students who are able and willing to pay extortionate fees coincidentally corresponding to those with the greatest academic ability? The main problem associated with this kind of 'internationalisation', namely corruption, made headlines in the British media in the summer of 2012. As we will see further on, the *Sunday Telegraph* named those UK universities, many of them quite well regarded, which – according to the Asian agent quoted by the newspaper – accept significantly lower grades from overseas students than from those eligible to pay mere domestic fees. In this way, the gap is widening between academic decision-making on the one hand, and on the other, both the university's representation of itself (as selling its product to the highest bidder) and even more importantly, its fashioning of students' expectations and of their self-perception as consumers.

RESEARCH AND HIGHER EDUCATION

Although most institutions of Higher Education are highly diverse and complex organisations, most fulfil both research and educational missions. Particular disciplines and particular systems or institutions may be more research-intensive than others, certainly. However, a spectrum extending from 'education, training and certification' on one end to 'blue sky' or 'open' searching at the other, is what generally distinguishes 'Higher' education. The educational responsibilities of more strictly vocational or professional Higher Education institutions are perhaps less complex or conflicted than those of more broadly academic ones. The latter typically have to juggle not only the often distinct imperatives of 'training' on the one hand and 'education' on the other, but also the more clearly diverging priorities of (commercially driven) 'research', on the one hand, and 'education' on the other. Whereas the distance between the 'training' and 'education' ends of the spectrum is relatively easy to measure, locating the best balance between research and education is much trickier.

There are many possible models for balancing these two priorities. The only general balance appropriate to an institution of Higher Education seems, though, to be one in which research/scholarship and teaching are both encouraged and valued in a manner wholly compatible with the institution's core 'Higher' educational mandate, namely, the enabling of informed, reflective and independent judgement in and between students/scholars of the various disciplines. This applies as much to the University of Chicago as to the various colleges of the National University of Ireland, even though the former is an almost exclusively research-oriented and private university teaching mostly graduates, whereas the NUI, a public university, educates undergraduates preponderantly.

In reality, however, with the rise of the competitive, output-driven university, it has become extremely difficult to maintain a balance between the two imperatives of research and teaching, especially, perhaps, in those disciplines where the research itself is very costly and where its commercialisation potential is extraordinary. Because of the contemporary emphasis on innovation as the key to commercial value, the custodial role and sometimes even the educational role of universities risk being neglected, especially where these cannot be commercialised through (mass-)education. As we will see, the exclusive identification of universities with the research mission is highly problematic. And this is so especially when the commercialisation – and/or the competitive measurement – of research becomes an end in itself and pulls almost completely away from the educational mission. This is indeed why, paradoxically, the research monopoly is blamed by some critics of the US education system for driving overall undergraduate educational standards into the ground. The challenge is, then, to find a way of integrating the demands of an explosion of commercially-driven 'research' with the demands of universal mass access to tertiary education.

Even if commercially-driven research has been allowed in some cases to smother undergraduate education, an 'equal and opposite' danger beckons if universities court the other extreme. This happens when, perhaps in response to external pressure or maybe in order to deflect attention from their less educationally-focused business interests, they launch management-led crusades involving ever more detailed and controlling demands for proof that an academic's research is having a direct and demonstrable impact on the content of their teaching. Far from guaranteeing improved educational 'results', such efforts to programme the relation between research/scholarship and teaching, however well-meaning, are almost certain, as we will see further on, to be educationally counter-productive. They risk removing the 'Higher' from 'Higher Education' and infantilising students and academics alike. Furthermore, they are likely to distract everybody from far bigger and more pervasive educational problems such as the real purpose of Higher Education and the vexed question of real academic standards.

FUNDING CORPORATE AMBITIONS

Contemporary threats to academic and intellectual values do not originate in sources either exclusively internal or exclusively external to the Higher Education sector itself. Instead, Higher Education institutions hold up a mirror to the wider social, political and economic environment in which they operate. Thus, some Irish corporate universities, like their international counterparts, appear to have 'grown' their overall 'business' to such monumental proportions that they are caught in the particularly vicious circle of a steadily worsening funding crisis. In the US, for example, traditional funding sources such as state governments (for the public universities), various private corporations and wealthy alumni are less and less able to afford to make the required investments. This situation has seen corporate universities internationally sealing various Faustian pacts with their 'sponsors', including in some cases their own clients, that is, students and their parents or other backers. The dramatic inflationary increases in tuition fees and in student and graduate debt both in the US and the UK speak volumes about the situation. There, as in Canada, Australia and even some continental European countries, public universities in particular are in dire straits financially and desperately seeking sponsors, such as the governments and students of the Gulf States and of Southeast Asia, most notably. In the next two sections, we will be looking more closely at some of these Higher Education connections and at the reputational risk and even moral hazard involved in, for example, the establishment of university branches, joint campuses or private medical schools in the most cash-rich parts of the world.

The commercial entanglements of today's corporate universities are incomparably diverse in terms of their implications, and indeed these implications can fluctuate dramatically over time. In today's world, but especially since 2008, the political, social and financial environments of most Western sources of external funding are enormously volatile. Hence, though it might seem preposterous to compare deals that have been made by Irish or other Western universities with the political regimes of Bahrain, Libya, China, Singapore or Malaysia, for example, and those struck with this or that biomedical giant, there is, in fact, a common denominator. Indeed, regardless of the incommensurable circumstances and stakes of all the funding entanglements mentioned throughout this book, the fundamental question remains the same. It concerns the freedom of Higher Education from the kind of political and economic compromises that could prevent them from being seen to pursue their core purpose independently. How can an academic institution uphold the basic standards of truthfulness or intellectual independence if it

is operating even partly under the auspices of interests prepared
to deny both values on the altar of power, prestige or profit? And
if these institutions cannot guarantee that the direct sponsors of
their activities will uphold the minimal standards upon which
the value of those activities is predicated, then to what extent
are they responsible when things unravel? The nightmare situation for a college, an individual academic or an academic team
is surely to discover, too late, that it has – however indirectly and
ingenuously – been co-opted or even bankrolled by forces or interests whose values conflict – sometimes dangerously and even
murderously – with those standards.

In May 2011 the new Chairman of Ireland's Higher Education
Authority was widely reported as castigating academics who
'hold their noses' at the idea of Higher Education working with
private industry. Media reports also described the HEA chair,
a former industrialist, as being 'particularly critical of the atti-
tudes of some academics teaching arts and humanities', an area
which, according to him, unlike the sciences, has difficulty in
communicating its contribution to the wider society. As we will
see, one of the most salient contributions of the humanities is
precisely to draw attention to the dangers long associated with
allowing political or economic expediency to over-ride critical
vigilance. This means, amongst other things, reminding human
beings, academics included, that they do have noses, even when
entire organisations, institutions and societies appear to be
sporting invisible clothes pegs. The humanities disciplines, for
example philosophy, history or cultural studies, exist in order to
make connections, to join the dots between certain choices and
certain consequences. As when the 'return to type' of a vindic-
tively repressive regime sells its friends and allies down the river,
including the foreign Higher Education institutions that had na-
ively cosied up to it. Or when a university finds that the pharma
company whose name is written all over its research funding is
prosecuted for criminal activities of which misrepresentation

and fraud are the least grievous. And, as we will see, because of its timing or because of the brutality of the symbolism, that particular stink-bomb wakes up academics and universities – for a time at least – to what they have become.

The (Irish) Higher Education Reform Fallacy

The picture painted here of the 'corporate university' does not at all correspond to the view of Higher Education reflected in the Irish media. Many regular or guest pundits tend to go along with the view that Irish academia is awash with overpaid academics whose ivory towers are intact, grossly undermanaged and smugly unrattled by contact with the 'real world'. There seems to be, indeed, a consensus that there is only one permissible question to be asked about Higher Education in Ireland (which is, how to reform it), and that the right answer to that question is increased regulation, increased accountability, heavy economic pruning and whatever it takes to achieve higher velocity (back) up the World League of corporate universities. So what is the non-insider to think? Is the educational integrity of Irish Higher Education under threat, and if so from which quarters? From academics bleating about a Shangri-La of outdated privileges such as tenure and academic freedom, which only serve to defend chronic waste and to protect wasters? But if that were so, then how come the US system, which has 'managed' over twenty years or so to shrink its proportion of tenured academics right down to a mere 30 per cent of all academic posts, appears to be experiencing such severe educational dysfunction? And what of those universities, near and far, that have 'managed' to divest themselves of the burden of 'loss-making' subjects such as Philosophy (periodically threatened in several UK universities), Physics, Geography and French (often targeted for the chop in the US), or Russian, Arabic, German and Hebrew (recently amputated in some Irish universities)? What have they got to show for this academic shearing, often cunningly disguised by 'folding' the 'redundant' subject into interdisciplinary programmes or service courses, in other words, into business that sells?

Could it possibly be that the core values of Higher Education, and hence its credibility and legitimacy, are more endangered than protected by those forces peddling a double mantra of competitive commercialisation and structural reform as silver bullets for the challenges faced by the sector worldwide? And could it be that it is precisely this type of business reform, rather than the alleged shortcomings of frontline academic labour, that has bloated parts of the sector's costs to popping point?

If ever an academic artist spoke truth to power in Ireland, it was when the newly appointed Ireland Professor of Poetry, the poet and teacher Harry Clifton, spoke at the announcement in 2010 of his three-year appointment. In his acceptance speech, Professor Clifton said that it was his intention to protect the sanctity of what he called the poet's 'teaching room' from 'the kind of people who have too strong an agenda'. He was to all appearances replying directly to the words of the then Taoiseach, Brian Cowen, who had just announced the poet's academic appointment. Mr Cowen had stated notably that the arts had a big role to play in getting Ireland 'back on track'. 'Ireland is a brand,' he had baldly observed. 'We must connect with that brand now and use it to give us the competitive advantage in a globalised world that is increasingly the same.' In his own forthright speech, Professor Clifton warned that if the 'teaching room' was opened too wide to the 'university ideologue, the modulariser, the smurfitiser, the harvardiser', the space would become, as he put it:

> . . . no more than a crush of market forces where the human mind becomes a commodity to be sold to the highest bidder. I think that is the terrifying thing and it's why teaching for me is a sacred activity. (*The Irish Times*, 1 July 2010)

The former Taoiseach's words had the merit of clearly demonstrating a truth if anything more valid and more stripped of moral fig-leaves in 2012 than in 2010 despite a change of government: namely, that the realm of politics has been taken over by the rootless, faceless and nameless market forces flowing through opaque channels all around the globe. The message could not be clearer: Irish Higher Education exists not to serve an ideal of human or social justice or fulfilment, but to sell Ireland Inc. for the highest price.

The systemic transformation of certain leading Irish Higher Education institutions into commercial operations is a done deed. Yet the shrill calls for rationalisation still regularly resounding via the Irish media suggest that non-insiders do not realise that the operating language of large swathes of third-level education – in Ireland as elsewhere – has been for some years the language of the 'modulariser, the smurfitiser, the harvardiser'. It is the impoverished, standardised and totalitarian language of business systems and structures, of market competition and ranking, of output growth and audit, of performance managerialism, of alignment to five-point strategic plans, of accountability to clients, sponsors and investors, of impact measurement and full economic costing, of downsizing and mergers, of privatisation and income generation. I suggest the term 'totalitarian' because of the anti-democratic and often intimidatory manner in which the usually quite silly propaganda of corporate university competitiveness has been bludgeoning 'Higher' educational ideals into silence. How does this vain and vacuous propaganda play out within the corporate universities so admired by those who would like to model all of Higher Education upon them?

FIVE LEGACIES OF THE BUSINESS REFORM OF EDUCATION

1. Branding Education, or the Wages of Spin

This book will quote from a great number of informed and authoritative sources who maintain that academics in the worldwide corporate system have substantively lost control over the integrity of Higher Education. If this is so, how did it happen?

In the US, the point has been made by some commentators that the notion of 'cheap mortgages' for all, home-owning nirvana at any price, the 'buy now, pay later or (on the) never-never', is strikingly similar to the discourse on Higher Education, where nobody thinks to question the commodity on offer as being a must-have at any price, regardless of astronomic levels of student and graduate debt. Educationalists will agree that no person should be deprived of the very best available education, including Higher Education, and especially not on material grounds, because they cannot afford to pay the monetary price. Equally, however, education as a human right should be authentically an education. It should not be a swindle. It should not be empty certification or credentialism masquerading as education. Indeed, the intrinsic, socially and individually transformative value of education should never be in question.

And yet, if, despite exponentially increased democratic access to formal Higher Education, and despite the revolutionary availability of knowledge allowed by technological advances, Higher Education is still functioning above all, right across the globalised world, as a proxy for (global) prestige, power and money, then academic values are as good as obsolete in that world. More specifically, if corporate academics come to feel that their role is pre-eminently commercial, and that they must not just hold their noses but also close their eyes to the political and economic injustice or dishonesty being served in some instances by their work, as well as to the intellectual and academic impoverishment

29

characterising the prevailing corporate ethos of far too many institutions, then Higher Education will surely have to start calling itself something else.

There may be a spectrum of opinion about the viability today (or ever) of an idealistic view of Higher Education as defending intrinsic, rather than exchange, values. But surely it is obvious that we cannot indefinitely deny that what we in the Global/Anglo world have been hiding behind, a two-way smokescreen of managerial and commercial gobbledegook, is – in many respects – a self-aggrandising, proxy-driven system. Indeed, because of the speed at which that system is now spinning, even those who argue in a spirit of pragmatic realism that continued spin is the only viable option are beginning to be more frank than they would hitherto have allowed themselves to be about the consequences. The views of one UK educational commentator, Roger Brown, are instructive in this respect. Brown is the former CEO of the UK's Higher Education Quality Council and currently co-directs the Centre of Higher Education Research Development at Liverpool Hope University. He is co-author and editor of *Higher Education and the Market*, published by Routledge in 2010. As quoted in a recent *Times Higher Education* article by Sarah Cunnane, Brown wants to alert the UK to the need to learn from mistakes made in Higher Education in the United States. In his book, he outlines the principles that he believes to be essential to ensuring that states and societies reap the benefits of Higher Education competition without the detriments. The top two principles on his list are sensible: first, 'in a diverse, mass system, there can be no single view as to what is meant by educational quality'; and second, that 'as far as the quality of university programmes and awards is concerned, the best protection still lies in the values and professionalism of the academic community'. What is striking, however, about the analysis presented by Brown in the paper quoted in the *THE* article is his reluctance to come straight out with the inevitable conclusion that Higher

Education is slouching ever closer towards make-believe. While his observations point to just that conclusion, he cannot name it directly. So, although he believes that universities cannot avoid 'rankings, business models or branding', he does not state the consequences of that powerlessness to change course. The strain inherent in Brown's position is particularly clear in the following statement:

> This is the schizophrenic position we're in: we're all engaged in a market at the same time as trying to provide education. You have to compromise, but you have to make those compromises without the loss of the educational side. Otherwise it's impossible to justify the privileges universities have such as relative autonomy and tax breaks and so on.

Most arresting of all, however, is Brown's eventual dismissal of university league tables as completely worthless:

> You can't ignore rankings, because you're in a market. If you're going to organise things along market lines then consumers have to have information about products. The fact that the information isn't worth the paper it's printed on doesn't matter.

It was worth waiting for that moment of rebellious truth-telling. But is Brown right in thinking that the meaninglessness of the marketing and ranking drivel doesn't matter? After all, how long until someone openly admits that other 'consumer information' about academic product – pricing, quality assurance reports, or even academic grades and degrees – is in certain circumstances 'not worth the paper it's printed on'? In other words, where does the deception or delusion begin and where does it end?

2. *Bureaucratic Bulge*

One of the recurring insider complaints about Higher Education worldwide is the level of bureaucracy allegedly strangling it. More precisely, insiders complain about the numbers of managers 'needed' in order to keep the brand improvement and market positioning of corporate universities turning over. These figures are such that, at certain Irish universities, non-academic positions are understood to outnumber academic posts by a ratio of three to two. If we look at the picture in the US, it does not seem all that different. A 2010 policy report for the US Goldwater Institute, called 'Administrative Bloat in Higher Education: The Real Reason for High Costs in Higher Education', associates the rise in university costs between 1993 and 2007 with a huge and disproportionate percentage increase in the hiring of administrator/ managers – an increase three times as great as the percentage increase in the enrolment of students and twice the percentage increase in the hiring of academics.

What do these administrator/managers administer or manage? Academics themselves continue to administer their students' academic activities and, since technology streamlined this labour, they are typically involved in routine tasks such as entering and managing student data (records, exam results, etc). Fortunately, key administrators still do provide crucial frontline and backroom support to academics and students, and no university could work without their input in a whole range of essential areas: librarianship, building and grounds management, student recruitment, registration and orientation, IT support, examinations, graduations, international exchanges, careers advice, counselling and so on. The corporate university system also involves, however, a multiplicity of commercial and management roles. These are spread across individual institutions and across overarching bodies. This layer of administration is responsible for strategising and PR, for packaging and selling the corporate product (for example, research and the 'student experience') and for managing 'product' development. According to Benjamin Ginsberg, whose book *The Fall of the Faculty: The Rise of the All-Administrative University and Why It Matters* appeared with Oxford University Press in 2011, the single most significant ailment of Higher Education is precisely the malignant growth of this commercial management cadre. Ginsberg teaches Political Science at Johns Hopkins University and has over forty years' experience between Johns Hopkins and Cornell. According to him, 'adminstrative blight' has been destroying academia for the past thirty years in the US. As we will see further on, it is difficult to disagree with his contention that bloated commercialist armies have indeed contributed to the marginalisation of academic concerns in the corporate university. However, the problem is highly intractable because of the figures: behind all these mushrooming roles stand lives and livelihoods.

In fact, though, Ginsberg reserves his most scathing criticism for the academics-turned-administrators whom he regards as quislings. But, while he excoriates all of these (one-time front-line) academics, he is somewhat less critical of the ones he calls 'deanlets' and 'deanlings'. For he does accept that, realistically, only the very most corrugated of constitutions are going to be able to hold the academic line to any significant extent under the prevailing pressures of the managerialist pyramid. The account given by Annette Kolodny of her purgatory as Dean of Humanities at the University of Arizona (in her book *Failing the Future*) suffices to confirm that point. Moreover, Kolodny's title clearly identifies the chief loser in the spread of 'administrative blight': not the tormented dean herself, nor her colleagues, but rather the educational 'future' which the humanities and the university are arguably there to safeguard.

3. *Leadership: A Disabled Function*

The technocrats of Higher Education are often referred to as 'leaders', though this is hardly an apt term today. The '-crat' suffix derives from the Greek word for power (*cratos*), but in fact Higher Education's technocrats are just as powerless as politicians in the face of contemporary market forces. Indeed, the current disarray of the most exposed Higher Education chiefs is directly proportional, it would seem, to the recklessness of their disinvestment, during better times, from core academic values. In many cases, all that remains now of the 'can do' corporate dream with which some university leaders might once have been identified is the 'can't undo' nightmare of what turned out to be a hastily purchased off-the-shelf Pandora's Box of inappropriate and often counter-productive corporate structures, processes and practices. In other words, many of Higher Educations's less prophetic figureheads are now stuck, along with their bodyguard and indeed their troops, whether loyal or mutinous, in what former University President James Garland calls – in his book *Saving Alma Mater* – the 'unhappy family' of Higher Education, a broken and broke family that nobody knows how to fix.

One small but symbolic measure of the wasteful corporate frenzy that took over Higher Education institutions is provided by the disproportionate remuneration awarded to the top managers of these institutions or of their various units. Far from being a uniquely Irish problem, disproportionate or off-scale remuneration for academic managers is a highly controversial issue further afield as well. Not everywhere, not in France, for example, but most strikingly perhaps in the US, top academic managers are still being paid huge salaries even as some state (that is, public) universities are tumbling towards insolvency. According to one of the most unforgiving of US Higher Education commentators, the former Yale academic William Deresiewicz (writing in *The Nation* in May 2011):

> Universities, like corporations, claim they need to pay the going rate for top talent. The argument is not only dubious – whom exactly are they competing with for the services of these managerial titans, aside from one an-

other? – it is beside the point. Academia is not supposed to be a place to get rich. If your ego can't survive on less than $200,000 a year (on top of the prestige of a university presidency), you need to find another line of work.

This matter of off-scale remuneration has proved particularly damaging in Higher Education on account of the 'because we're worth it' argument typically used to justify it. Such self-belief is, of course, embarrassingly incompatible with the mess into which many of the most corporate Higher Education institutions worldwide have (been) sleepwalked. More specifically, it exposes the grandiose corporate dream of Higher Education as the stuff of fairly tales. It is no more real than the Emperor's new suit and no more salutary than the piping of the Hamelin charmer. In the withering words of Deriecewicz again – this time published in *The American Scholar*:

> Leadership means finding a new direction, not simply putting yourself at the front of the herd that's heading toward the cliff.

In a widely-noted and rather more heartbroken than bitter open letter addressed in June 2012 to his university colleagues, David Dudley, chair of the department of Literature and Philosophy at Georgia Southern University, also refers to the crisis of leadership threatening to engulf the 'university that I love'.

> I keep hearing that the current administration bears a dismissive and contemptuous attitude toward faculty [ie. academics]. From what I observe, there is truth in this observation. To my mind, this is the [most] fundamental mistake any university administration can make. Deans, provosts, and presidents come and go. Many such individuals are building their careers and are often looking to go on to the next, better job.... Georgia Southern has a long tradition of faculty members devoting their entire careers to this place. [It] belongs to its faculty and

staff every bit as much as it belongs to any administrator. In fact, it belongs more to us, because when the current deans and higher administrators are long gone, we will still be here, striving to maintain what this place stands for: individual attention to our students, which is why they come here.

Some universities are more fortunate both in their lead administrators and in their ability to recognise and defend the kind of leadership they can trust and respect. Thus, in mid-2012, when the President of the University of Virginia appeared to have been ousted by a boardroom coup – ostensibly for not driving the corporate agenda hard enough – academics and students fought back and had her reinstated.

4. *Managerialism and its Discontents*

The Irish Higher Education 'bonus bonanza' is only one small but visible example of the extravagance of the new 'executive' culture ushered in by university reform. Apart from the waste associated with the development of entirely new, busy-work managerial layers, there are other, bigger but less immediately visible problems linked to the sticky web of surveillance that has been spun in order to make universities look like real corporations, complete with impressive-sounding quality audit regimes. Firstly, the audit culture can leave – and in the Irish university bonus affair, it clearly did leave – major systemic irregularities such as unlawful bonuses and incentives untouched and untroubled. If an audit regime is exposed in this way, then it will rightly be treated as a charade. Secondly, audit regimes tend to encourage cultures of compliance and even conformity. As such, they are scarcely compatible with respect for critical or creative independence of spirit. Thirdly, unless they are very carefully handled, audit cultures can generate some of the most irreversible pathologies of what Francis Fukuyama called 'low-trust societies'. For example, elevated levels of guard labour. According to the former Harvard economist Samuel Bowles, intensive enforcement is typical of low-trust societies and the associated costs are appallingly high whether we look at bigger or smaller social contexts. The state of California, for example, home to what used to be the most respected and admired public university system in the US (including universities such as UCLA and Berkeley), was spending in 2010 45 per cent more money on its penitentiary system (11 per cent of budget) than on its Higher Education system (7.5 per cent of budget). In the corporate university, academic policing involves, as we will see, the deployment of extensive enforcement systems such as employee performance management, workload models, teaching feedback monitoring and 'total quality control' plus 'full economic costing' systems for all academic activities including research, teaching/learning, administration and so on. In academia, the primary concern is less, perhaps, the economic cost, than the diversion of resources from academic work and the fact that creativity audits both bespeak and reinforce a fundamental lack of understanding of, and trust in, academic work.

One of the more serious problems with the corporate Higher Education model is, then, its sheer incompatibility with the university's primary academic mission. As this book will show, education is based on a fabric of trust and legitimacy which is easy to destroy and difficult to rebuild. When that fabric was ripped apart by Thatcherism in 1980s Britain, Conrad Russell, the son of the famous philosopher Bertrand Russell, was able to be quite categorical about the fall-out for academic morale and self-respect:

> The idea of academic freedom must involve some sphere of autonomous professional judgment. There must be some things recognised as academic questions, to be decided by academics according to academic standards. It is this sphere which is now being whittled away to nothing. . . . If we cannot decide how to teach, what the

standard of the degree should be, what its justification and purpose are, or whether students are good enough to be admitted, what academic freedom do we have left? Professionals must have standards: without them, both grounds of self-respect and utility to society disappear. If, one after another, every one of these standards must be sacrificed on the altar of 'efficiency', what sort of professionals do we have left when the job is done? Almost everything academics are now asked to do, most of them believe to be wrong. Even if they are in error in that belief (and the possibility must be admitted), as long as they hold it, in conscience they ought to act on it. If they do not, their claim to society's respect, and indeed to their own, is forfeit. No one who has lost his professional self-respect can long remain good at his job. (*Academic Freedom*, from the epilogue written in 1992)

It is difficult to disagree with Russell's assessment of the academic consequences of the managerialist culture that still reigns supreme, not just over UK academia but also over whichever other systems adopted it (from Australia to Singapore to Canada to Ireland and now, apparently, US public universities too). Twenty-five years on from the UK reforms, its ever more embedded promotion of image over substance still feels all wrong.

5. Reforming or Deforming the Role of Academics: Performing or Conforming?

A fifth legacy of the commercial reform of Higher Education, arguably more far-reaching than any of the others, merits particular attention: namely, a reconfiguration of the role of the academic.

Nobody could deny that academics have a poor press generally. After all, when we want to dismiss a question as irrelevant, we say, 'It's academic', meaning it's neither here nor there. In her recent book, *Faculty Towers*, an overview of the comic 'campus novel' made famous by the likes of David Lodge and Malcolm

Bradbury, Elaine Showalter describes the academic stereotype very well, and with special reference to Kingsley Amis's masterpiece of the fifties, *Lucky Jim*. Showalter writes that 'the book portrays professors as stuffy, ridiculous phoneys, whose confidence is complacency and whose self-importance is matched only by their insignificance'.

Things (not least the sexism) have changed a lot in academia since Kingsley Amis filleted its foibles. Yet academics are still widely supposed to be change-averse, dogmatic, impractical and out of touch; in other words, impossible to manage. Furthermore, certain Irish media outlets have lately developed a new niche market for articles knocking them – along with teachers – for a whole new set of reasons. Now, in Ireland at least, academics are regularly portrayed in the press, for example, as spoiled, lazy, greedy, over-rated, under-scrutinised and over-priced.

In my experience, today's academics are anything but 'unmanageable'. And whether that is a good or a bad thing is, as we may see, debatable. Concerning the charges of being grasping and work-shy, however, these are very new accusations and particularly prevalent in Ireland. As such, they beg two questions. What is the basis of this impression of (Irish) academia? And whose interests is it serving? It is difficult not to link it to a series of public statements by some senior Higher Education figures as reported in the national media. I am thinking of the public defense of (in some cases wildly) off-scale salaries for some top university managers, who were declared in one memorable *Irish Times* interview to be modern-day King Midas figures, wizards of (research or tuition) income generation. Unfortunately, well before those words were inked, the economic low pressure zones that had precipitated euro-rain into Ireland's academic watertanks were already disappearing. There have also been media reports of public comments by authorities such as senior figures of this or that Higher Education body or quango about allegedly untouchable rogue academics who rarely do a day's work, and about academics in general having lost public trust and respect. Such friendly fire has undoubtedly done much to give credence to the negative image of rank and file academics which permeates public discourse on Irish Higher Education. There will be a fuller discussion of this issue in section 3, but it is important to clarify the matter of off-scale academic remuneration immediately, because of its urgency at a time when all areas of the Irish education system are struggling to be adequately resourced.

First of all, with the notable exception of some medical consultants also employed as university academics, off-scale academic remuneration is, and performance bonuses were apparently (when they were still being paid), confined to the managerial or administrative cadre within Higher Education. Furthermore, at least one of the universities which authorised the bonuses in question has explicitly and unambiguously recognised *not just* that these were only paid to academics serving as university officers (often heading up academic units), but also that they were paid solely to reward or to incentivise income generation. As such, they relate exclusively, by that university's own explicit admission, to *commercial targets and activities*. Furthermore, they had strictly nothing to do with the scaled incomes of frontline academics, or indeed with the *specifically academic work* for which those frontline academics are paid scaled and benchmarked salaries. Second, it is surely impossible to defend such bonuses or allowances – certainly on the basis that they reward or incentivise *commercial* performance – without tacitly accepting the systemic engulfing, not to say perversion or corruption, of academic values by commercial ones.

In considering more generally what academic Armageddon has done to Higher Education in Ireland and in the wider world, we will see that, regardless of whether they are paragons of public virtue, or self-serving delinquents, or else somewhere in the middle, the real problem is that neither front-line academics, nor university managers or leaders, nor even government or state agencies are actually 'in charge' of the direction being taken by Irish Higher Education. In fact, whether Higher Education as a public good will survive Armageddon or not will depend not on the intellectual reach or ethical backbone of academics and administrators (individually or collectively), nor even on the values of the sector's 'steering columns', but rather on our whole society's understanding and expectations of Higher Education. As a system, it will not be better than what we as a society expect and hope for – for ourselves and for posterity.

THE ACADEMIC EMPLOYEE AND INTELLECTUAL FREEDOM: CORPORATE SILO-BUSTING

Academics are rightly expected to be at the 'cutting edge' both of knowledge and of ideas. Rather than simply preserving and transmitting a body of supposedly established and static 'knowledge', they are legitimately supposed to challenge the limits of current understanding. Above all, they are expected to share with their students an appreciation of learning and questioning as a permanent way of life, rather than just as a three-year college hiatus. What do academics have to be in order to fulfill this mandate? Clearly, they must be more than just specialists; they must want to, and must be able and free to, stress-test not just 'knowledge' but also language, power, dogma and so on.

Before the clear political divide between Left and Right came to a sticky end, academics were often identified with the conservative, bourgeois Right; intellectuals with the radical, revolutionary Left. After the 'cultural revolution' of the sixties, that cliché no longer held in the West. And following the collapse of state Communism, the universal preference has been for academics served up in the politically neutral sauce of saleable expertise. So today academics are required to function not as free-roaming intellectuals but rather as the specialised farmers of a relatively restricted field of knowledge, or even as the game- or gate-keepers of intellectual property.

There can be a considerable amount of tension surrounding what academics probably regard as their chief responsibility, namely, the requirement to think critically, independently and creatively. Top of the list of pressures working against that responsibility are the twin imperatives of our inflationary and accelerative age – King Growth and Queen Speed. These forces have taken over universities governed by the UK managerialist model of 'productivity'. They have been putting academics, particularly those less far advanced into their careers, under artificial, counterproductive and damaging pressure to produce intellectual property for their employers. Put simply, if it takes time to think, it takes ages to think critically, independently and creatively, even in a small way. But far more dramatic, in fact, than either the pressure of growth or acceleration is the requirement to comply with certain commercial and/or managerialist imperatives, even when these actually decimate not just critical and creative thinking, but even truth and honesty.

Of all the possible examples of this destructiveness, the language of the so-called 'research excellence framework' which currently sets the agenda for academic research in UK universities is probably the most astonishing. In an article published in *Times Higher Education* in June 2012, Fred Inglis, Honorary Professor of Cultural History at the University of Warwick, lambasts the framework's language as 'revolting', 'fatuous', 'flatulent', 'inane', 'intellectually grotesque', 'venally thoughtless' and 'mendacious'. Inglis further suggests that the REF, which directs the measurement of research activity at UK universities, is reproduced rather than challenged by those universities which plaster silly advertising slogans and self-aggrandising straplines across their websites and their job advertisements. And he recalls George Orwell's observation on the problem with all such strategic or 'political' language, namely, that it is 'designed to make lies sound truthful and murder respectable, and to give an appearance of solidity to pure wind'. Fred Inglis claims that 'every [academic] department' in the UK 'is united in the incredulous contempt' in which it holds the language and machinery of the REF. Unfortunately, however, that contempt is not translated into revolt. Both in and beyond the UK, academics seem to be swallowing whatever contempt they may feel, and playing along with charades.

Another clear example of the ways in which the work of academics is being demeaned by the current commercialist orientation of Higher Education concerns the delicate matter of academic freedom. In corporate management 'lone trading' and 'silo working' are not terms of endearment. Like the ivory tower, the silo is a tall cylindrical structure. And in the business world, silos are a byword for protectionist isolation, and thereby for inefficiency. On the whole, today's corporate universities are intent upon demolishing silos and towers, and the result is often a sad and apparently irreversible flattening of the academic landscape. It would be surprising if this leveling didn't result in a world where all too often the bland are leading the bland. In other words, the very last place where one would look for the kind of thinking that is truly independent, unforced and original. Of course, it is true that, in some cases, inter-disciplinary, team-led research might make eminent sense, as might research on pre-ordained themes or so-called strategic research. However, in other cases or disciplines, especially disciplines where academic activity only requires brain-space and brain-time for individuals and does not necessitate vast sums of money, the whole point of the exercise is about imagining new areas, themes or questions. Deciding which questions are worth examining and how they might best be examined is indeed the fundamental role of academic work as a whole.

Important as it might be to make room for un-programmed, non-formatted research and for the eccentric, original mind, an even bigger problem with the tower-toppling, silo-busting approach is that it is increasingly imposed in the corporate university, not just upon research, but also upon what is taught or what students study. 'Multidisciplinarity' and 'interdisciplinarity' are the new magic words of the contemporary 'Higher' curriculum. Wave them about and hey presto, there's a shortcut, via 'synergies', to 'creativity', 'critique' and 'innovation'. In certain fields or at certain levels of activity, and especially when individual academics and individual disciplines are also respected and nurtured in themselves, collaborative and interdisciplinary openings are no doubt beneficial. But just as 'international' implies separate nations, so too the very notion of 'interdisciplinarity' is based on separate disciplines. If over-systematically applied, or over-instrumentalised, the doctrine of interdisciplinarity can damage the integrity of individual disciplines, distracting students and teachers from the elemental cores, in all their depth and detail. As such that doctrine would make about as much sense in Higher Education as 'abolishing' or 'diluting' discrete and crucial disciplines such as history as core subjects at second level. As we will see further on, the development of radically interdisciplinary models of Higher Education is accelerating, but it is highly questionable as a model for undergraduate or postgraduate education across the board.

Academic Freedom/Academic Responsibility: Two Sides of the Same Coin

There is a further reason for not requiring academics to drive their research work across disciplinary boundaries (as per the terms of what purports to be a binding contract sent to the academic employees of certain Irish universities in mid-July 2012). Namely, the fact that, unless they are the sole academic representing a given discipline in a given institution, or unless their teaching is confined to very specialised or even post-graduate courses, academics must of necessity collaborate with their col-

leagues in co-teaching a balanced and varied undergraduate curriculum or programme, and it is only in their research that they
can really extend themselves fully to their academic limits.

The freedom of academic manoeuvre is thus 'naturally' cor-
ralled by many entirely legitimate factors. It is limited by academics' responsibilities to their students, undergraduates as
well as graduates; by their responsibilities to their colleagues; by
their responsibility to the integrity and scope of their discipline;
and by their intellectual and ethical responsibilities to the wider
academic community and to society and humanity as a whole.
As this book clearly shows, academic freedom is above all the
freedom to be true to all of those responsibilities. The problem,
however, is that the extra demands made of academics by the
corporate university conflict more and more with 'academic freedom', and they do so precisely because they prevent academics
from discharging core academic responsibilities. These anti-academic demands include requirements to work across disciplines
as well as (or rather than) within their home discipline and/or
to direct their research towards areas or themes pre-selected by
their employer or by national or transnational funding agencies.
But they can also include commercially-driven requirements to
increase student enrollment, more especially to meet targets of
overseas or postgraduate recruitment; requirements to increase
the numbers of students retained or graduated by the university;
requirements to increase research outputs; to accelerate research
results; to expedite academic decisions in circumstances where
proper administrative support has been reduced or withdrawn;
or requirements to tailor course content and standards to elicit
favourable 'customer satisfaction' ratings.

The problem is not that the corporate university's business
plan will cramp the style of pampered academic egos. Yes, many
corporate imperatives will strain and even break some of the
sancrosanct principles of academic work. But even worse, in
some, if not many or even all cases, these requirements will run

directly counter to the academic's better judgment of their academic duty and principles.

Armageddon could never have happened had academic responsibilities not been re-formatted by the spiraling and conflicting demands enumerated above. To be clear: some professional tension is of course inevitable and even productive between academic freedom and academic responsibilities. An obvious example is the need to juggle roles both as cutting-edge specialists in very narrow domains and also as broadly critical and creative lateral thinkers. Or the need to combine high-level research and scholarship, while simultaneously giving of one's best to bread-and-butter undergraduate education, particularly in the all-important first undergraduate year. But there is an obvious difference between those inevitable tensions that 'go with the territory' and the double bind into which the corporate university has strapped its academics. For today's corporate academics, the dilemma is how to operate simultaneously as radically questioning minds and as compliant transmission belts for the implementation of strategic plans and targets that have never been openly debated and that may in fact conflict with fundamental educational principles, not to mention with other vital elements of the public good.

The fact is that today's academics are being pressured as never before to scale ever higher heights of academic 'productivity'. Whatever one thinks about this pressure, one of its main effects is crystal clear. It necessarily prevents most academics from having the mental energy necessary to stress-test morally and intellectually the goals set for them by technocracies whose subservience to markets marks those goals with a deep democratic deficit. How could individual academics stand up to such forces? Well, as this book will show, if ever a question were purely 'academic', it is this one. As we will see, a recent American court case and an ongoing attempt to revise Irish academic contracts seem to suggest that, if in the future US or Irish academics do have qualms about the overall direction being taken by Higher Education, then they will have to choose between their conscience and their jobs.

THE TAME ACADEMY HISTORICALLY

Non-academic intellectuals, those journalists and writers not directly involved in education, for example, are more easily tolerated by society than their academic peers. For one thing, they don't 'come with' decades of professional protectionism and self-insulation. And for another, they don't cost even a nano-fraction of the wages of academic intellectuals. In fact, in these recessionary times, even flagship Western democracies can almost be heard wondering if they can afford the apparent luxury of 'kept' thinkers. Those academics necessary as trainers for the economy will always be thought necessary, although smart economies will hire them as cheaply as possible and exclusively for focusing on their area of expertise. Indeed, it is probably inevitable that such societies will rationalise ever further their Higher Education institutions into commercial, credentialising outfits producing certified graduates of 'whatever is expected to be useful to the national economy'.

Yet such strategic rationalisation is a gamble that could prove costly if the future takes an unexpected turn, as futures tend to do. More importantly, however, the promotion of training at the expense of education is the indisputable hallmark of an unfree society. We already know what Higher Education systems look like when they focus exclusively on narrowly servicing the current national economic interest. The Soviet Union boasted just such a system. Indeed, a recent book edited by Brendan Walsh, *Degrees of Nonsense*, explicitly attributes 'the demise of the university in Ireland' to what it calls the 'neo-Soviet' approach to Higher Education. However, even those societies that maintain a less utilitarian view of education, but that find other ways of neutralising or muting independent academics, are also un-free.

Hostility towards thinkers with the potential (if not the vocation or explicit mission, even) to question 'received wisdom' or to critique the status quo is nothing new. Indeed, in one of the most viciously genocidal of communist revolutions, hostility was specifically directed at those assumed to be educated or academic. This is why bespectacled people – presumed to have ruined their eyesight by too much study – were shot and/or decapitated on sight by the Khmer Rouge. Paradoxically, Marxism, or the 'science of proletarian revolution', was invented by middle class intellectuals. But from China to Cambodia to the Soviet Union, state Communism was to prove murderously hostile to the studiously or intellectually independent beings whose very existence was perceived as an affront, if not a threat, to totalitarianism.

It is, of course, a fact that, from Argentina's 1960s generals to Burma's current military dictators, and from Hitler's to Stalin's to Mussolini's to Franco's to Salazar's to the Al Khalifa or Tiananmen Square versions of totalitarianism, from Mao's cultural revolution to Iran's theocracy, none of today's or yesteryear's repressive regimes have failed to find academics willing to staff the Higher Education establishments run under their auspices. How difficult was it for Nazi Germany to replace the Jewish academics whom it evicted from its universities? In the face of the bleak answer to that question, academics can only recognise in all humility that the academy is, above all else, a place of conformity. Even so, some small, if grim comfort can be taken from the purges, intimidation and censorship sometimes required in order to keep a lid on its intellectual independence. Thus, Iran had to close its universities for a time in 1980, pending attempted curricular purification. And Argentina's General Onganía, one month after the coup that installed him, had the Faculties of Science at the University of Buenos Aires stormed by police on the 'Night of the Long Police Batons'. Professors and students were attacked and imprisoned and an extensive brain drain ensued.

Similar attempts at academic cleansing include the McCarthyist purges of supposed Reds. More recent targetings of academics include the attempted silencing of those who spoke out against various 'Homeland Security' excesses in the wake of 9/11 and the 2011 dismissal – according to Human Rights Watch – of academics from Bahrain's Higher Education institutions following so-called 'Arab Spring' pro-democratic unrest. All these examples illustrate the validity of academic and intellectual freedom as barometers of ambient social and political freedom.

THE TAME ACADEMY TODAY

Although it is relatively rare, published evidence of a conservative backlash against academic freedom in contemporary Western democracies could perhaps be seen as proof of a freely independent Higher Education system, but on closer inspection this appears to be wishful thinking. There have been signs of a backlash, but its importance is dwarfed by the real dangers currently facing academic freedom and integrity. In 2006, in *The Professors: The 101 Most Dangerous Academics in the US*, author David Horowitz claims that there is a pervasive and insidious liberal bias at American universities which is taking what he calls coercive anti-American, anti-religion, left-wing politics into the classroom. Horowitz is outraged by what he views as a conspiracy of ideologues who are allegedly abusing academic freedom as a front for anti-war activism, feminism, socialism, political correctness, climate change theory, and so on. He is so infuriated, indeed, that he has drawn up an 'Academic Bill of Rights' to defend students oppressed by the academics who peddle these 'dangerous ideologies' in the classroom. The book received significant levels of publicity in the US. Charles McGrath, reviewing it for the *New York Times* in November 2006, points out that Horowitz's case studies contain a disproportionate number of Humanities professors in a country where Humanities students are a dramatically dwindling category:

49

> If indeed there is a professorial cabal dedicated to con-
> verting American students to Marxism, or worse, it is
> manifestly failing. The country is more conservative than
> it has been in decades, and by far the most popular un-
> dergraduate major these days is business.

McGrath's review is entitled 'A Liberal Education? Depends on
Who's Looking'.

Before congratulating today's corporate universities on being
such havens of intellectual independence that they have given
rise to sporadic outbreaks of neocon rage, we should think about
how a commercial Higher Education model can accommodate
meaningful intellectual freedom. How can we expect genuine
intellectual independence to be respected in the 'Higher Education' provision demanded by societies where 'freedom' has been
reduced to consumer choice between more or less affordable educational brands and more or less favourable student mortgage
or loan rates?

It is entirely possible that academic freedom is, by and large,
just as alive and kicking in Iran, Singapore, Malaysia, China and
Bahrain as it is in any university in the US, the UK, France or
Ireland. If so, that just goes to show how purely 'academic' such
'freedom' is. The fact is that few universities worldwide currently
fail to write 'academic freedom' into their mission statements
and operating policies, along with a plethora of other politically
correct genuflexions to all the usual contemporary ideals such
as dignity, fairness and equality of opportunity in the academic workplace. And yet, in corporate colleges worldwide there is
increasingly a sense in which academic freedom has become a
purely academic question (in the worst sense). So why are many
academics not at all reassured by their administration's lip service to academic freedom? Why are they not duly grateful for
their handlers' pious assertions of their 'right' or 'freedom' to determine what they teach, write, profess or research within their
area of academic 'expertise'? Well, probably because they know

that such freedom is worthless if they cannot stand over the ethos, the structures or the processes of the system within which they carry out their teaching or research. For example, if I work in a UK public university that requires students to indebt themselves to the yearly tune of £9,000 to study for a primary degree, where does that leave my educationalist credibility? Or if I work in an American or Irish public university where academic staff are hired, retained, promoted or remunerated at least partly on the basis of the tuition-fee or research-grant income that they attract to the university? Or if pressure to retain students is obliging academics to drop standards? Or if student feedback exerts such tyranny that individual academics are accused of putting 'their' students at an advantage if they expose them to material over and above that prescribed in the 'module descriptor'? And what of academics working in universities so entirely 'on message' that any divergence, public or not, from pseudo-neutral 'strategic plans' aligned on the 'national economic interest' will be censured not just as anti-patriotic but as outright economic treason in a state of economic 'Emergency'?

There is at least one fundamental and fatal flaw in the Brave New World of the corporate university as a purely economic global driver, and much of this book is devoted to illustrating it. Until such time as humanity has solved all the problems facing it globally (starvation, climate disaster, the arms trade, nuclear threat, tribalism, sexual violence, epidemics, internecine warfare, forced displacement, urban slums, child neglect, exploitation and mortality – as in the daily deaths of 4,000 children from water-borne disease), societies and economies do not just need well-trained consumers, tax payers and debt reimbursers, but also trustworthy sources of genuinely critical, independent and humane thinking. This means a kind of thinking that is free, open and informed enough to be genuinely able to relativise its own here and now. If 'education' by historically and culturally blinkered immersion in group-think just won't do, if we are to avoid a situation where 'Higher Education' boils down to the reproduction of captive minds, then all roads lead to the necessity of making room for ceaseless questioning and divergence. Not just in the classroom, however. It has to happen in and around the college boardrooms too. There is no plausible substitute for constant and informed, open and multilateral critique of the status quo, and especially of the relations prevailing institutionally between power, justice and knowledge. The idea of university administrations selling their employees' performance of critical thinking or, even worse, micro-managing their employees' delivery of 'modules in independent thinking' to student-clients, is worse than daft; it is a perfect oxymoron. And it blows the cover entirely off the academic fraud being perpetrated in the worst examples of the corporate rendition of Higher Education.

What are the concrete signs of a tame academy? If universities are trying to dispense altogether with thinking that would be 'open' to questioning and uncertainty, we would expect them to undervalue those disciplines that might serve to *relativise* the 'here and now' business imperatives of Higher Education speculation. And isn't this exactly what has been happening? Universities near and far, in the UK and US for example, have been closing down their departments of philosophy – the very subject that studies what knowledge or thought is – and they have also been closing their departments of classics and ancient languages and of modern languages such as Russian, German, Italian and Arabic. Only languages and cultures such as English and Chinese that can be held up as being immediately useful for, and in tune with, the only game in town – namely, global economic competition – have had a free pass. This anti-academic and opportunistic short-termism could be seen at work in Ireland long before the ink was fully dry on the death certificate of the Irish boom.

In some cases, anti-academic myopia smote most menacingly at the height of the bubble. In the mid-noughties, for example, it struck in an eventually aborted plan to abolish the possibility of degree-level study of Old Irish in one Irish university, and that plan was followed up by a similarly aborted initiative to convert a 'state of the art' Language Centre into an administrative suite for the same university's globalisation ventures. Reason prevailed in both cases, but in others the pressures were too severe. Thus, in 2006 the only Irish university offering degree-level study of Arabic terminated this service, along with degree-level Hebrew. When we consider the economic and political importance of the Near and Middle East in the current world order, and add to them all the reasons why a Western university would want to cherish the ethical, political and cultural openings enabled by advanced study of Arabic and Hebrew, these closures and others like them make no sense intellectually or educationally. The study of languages refines cross-cultural sensitivity. It offers a deep, almost internal view of how the world – and how world relations – appear through the lense of a different tongue. According to the new 'global gospel' of Higher Education, however, there is only one globe. And there is only one way of looking at it (as a market for lucrative overseas students) and only one way of talking to it (in the language of money). Hence we don't need to bother any more about in-depth study of 'irrelevancies' such as the languages of art, culture or thought. Although usually Higher Education's side-lining or eviction of certain subjects – particularly but not exclusively languages – is motivated not by educational concerns but by the conclusion that they are 'loss-making', there is sometimes a sense also that they are useless or irrelevant, that is, 'academic' in the worst sense, like Latin or Greek. There may even be a sense that 'purely' academic subjects implicitly challenge the simplified view of the globe as a market. Isn't this precisely why Geography currently appears to be under almost as much threat as French in US Higher Education, and why some quite reputable universities have also been threatening to target philosophy (Keele and Middlesex in the UK, Howard in the US) or even physics (Reading in the UK axed physics in 2006, while there are rumblings about getting rid of it in some state universities in both Texas and Florida).

Although languages as academic subjects are not beloved of the corporate university, those languages that can be bought and sold – not as academic subjects worthy of in-depth study, but rather as hard global currency – are, of course, cherished. The teaching of English as a foreign language, for example, has proved lucrative in Ireland as elsewhere in the Anglo Higher Education world. And although the TEFL market (Teaching English as a Foreign Language) may have been cornered by private or at least for-profit language schools on or off-campus, the teaching of Chinese has been spearheaded in general, and not just in Anglo-land, from within those universities which are most receptive to the Chinese government's love-bombing. It is not just in Ireland that universities have been trying to gain a competitive advantage by setting speed-dating records with Chinese partner institutions and by introducing partly 'bought-in', but mostly 'gifted' Chinese modules, into their degree programmes. Where Chinese is treated as an academic subject and where it is taught and examined in line with the same authentically academic standards as other subjects, then its programming is a positive educational development. Where these conditions do not fully apply, however, the screw tightens further, as we will see, on the coffin of the host's academic legitimacy.

As J.M. Coetzee and Bill Readings both suggest, so-called reformed universities are in reality re-formatted as business corporations. And as any undergraduate business textbook shows, business corporations are generally owned by, and accountable to, shareholders and are driven by market forces. They are (supposedly) managed to supply maximum market profit or benefit to their shareholders. In fact, however, it is sometimes difficult to determine the relative benefit really accruing to the various players in the corporate game. After all, many corporations (banks, for example) have been functioning more like agglomerations of highly mobile and opaque – if not ownerless – capital, which is controlled by, speculated upon, and even subjected to the interests of, a managerial oligarchy. This latter model seems to be a better match for the corporate university, whose dominant 'stakeholders' resemble shareholders insofar as they invest their own money in the institution, as fee-paying students or as public or private funders and sponsors. In other words, the corporate university may be ultimately driven by the commercial interests and demands of its clients and sponsors, rather than by specifically educational concerns. Of course there can be a perfect alignment between the two sets of interests and values. But we will see that there is currently a high risk of worldwide subordination of inherent educational priorities, not just to anonymous and undirected market forces, but also to political or business interests that, while they may not necessarily be profiteering or predatory, often run counter to concerns both for fundamental intellectual values and for broader imperatives such as educational equity and justice.

Irish 'Higher' Education: Re-writing the Academic Contract

Is real academic independence becoming a dead letter nowadays, even in the USA, the 'land of the free'? This certainly appears to be so, at least insofar as any real questioning of the running of universities is concerned. Ellen Schrecker begins her book *The Lost Soul of Higher Education* with a story. It concerns a case taken by an engineering academic against retaliatory measures invoked against him by the University of California at Irvine. He had challenged what he alleged to be serious irregularities in the running of the department in which he was employed, including the hiring of academics who had allegedly falsified their qualifications and the alleged abuse of 'perma-temp' contracts. The university had responded by measures that he regarded as retaliatory and he had sued. The first court found for the university on the grounds that First Amendment protection (of free speech) did not apply to the employee's raising of issues of university governance or management policies and operations. The actual judgment reads:

> . . . when public employees make statements . . . pursuant to their official duties, the Constitution does not insulate their communications from employer discipline.

Of course had this employee's 'disciplining' by the university related to his teaching or scholarship, then his words or actions would have been protected against sanction by the principle of academic freedom. The Association of University Professors immediately lodged a third-party – or *amicus curiae* – brief to appeal the first finding, since if the latter were to be upheld, academics (employed in state universities) who challenged their employers' modus operandi would no longer be legally protected from employer retaliation.

Although the appeal outcome was not known when Ellen Schrecker wrote her book (it failed, in fact), she uses this case to show that the US state will not protect individual academics who denounce what they regard as institutional abuses of power. Academic freedom may protect them if, for example, as academic experts in zoology they teach creationism or as academic historians write a (putatively scholarly) negationist article denying the facts of the Nazi genocide. But, should they denounce governance or administrative abuses, they will not be protected by any kind of immunity – not by their academic contracts, not by academic freedom principles or legislation and not (even) by the First Amendment. As the Senior Counsel for the AAUP put it, the failure of the appeal means that the expressive independence of academics (or at least the free speech of academics employed by public universities regarding the running of those universities) is actually less protected 'than that of the average American'.

To relate these matters to the current Irish context, we could glance at the Higher Education fallout from the 2010 Public Service (or Croke Park) Agreement. Broadly, the terms hammered out in the dying days of Ireland's last government constitute a Faustian pact. They ostensibly promise – in return for no more pay cuts and no job losses – more stringent managerial policing of academic 'productivity'. When the universities produced the Higher Education implementation plans which spelled out what that policing would involve, there were many predictable measures. Indeed, some of these, such as workload models, 'full economic costing' of academic work practices, and other performance and quality management processes, had been in place in many parts of Irish Higher Education for variable numbers of years prior to Croke Park. However, the proposals expressed such a radical distrust of academics, and such a profound misunderstanding of the nature of academic work, that they prompted a crystal-clear warning from the General Secretary of the Irish Federation of University Teachers (IFUT). They would, he declared, 'destroy the whole concept of a university'. He went on to say:

> They are so bad, that I really wonder if the university authorities at the highest level are even aware of [them] because, if by some miracle [IFUT] were to agree to them, it would no longer be a university as understood in any country in the world.

Unfortunately, there was, apparently, a miracle since the scarcely modified proposals have magically migrated via some as yet unclarified form of 'negotiation' and 'agreement' into a new academic 'contract' issued unilaterally in mid-July 2012 to the academics of at least one Irish university.

Apart from the new meaning given to the word 'contract' by an unagreed, unsigned, vague and incoherent document sent to all academic staff by email, the most important dimension of this development is the implausible 'make believe' version of academia that it has been found necessary to invent, apparently to placate both public opinion and the 'markets'. If, by some further miracle, this 'make believe' were to be taken seriously, however, it would represent an assault, not at all on the sectional interests of academics, but rather on core educational principles and values, and thereby on the general public interest.

I will return to this question of the public good in Section 3, but for now one point alone needs to be made. Pre-Armageddon, in Higher Education in general (not just in Ireland), academics could be, and were, disciplined up to and including dismissal, but not without 'just cause'. That 'just cause', wherever and whenever it was defined, involved a failure to uphold academic principles or to discharge their specifically academic responsibilities to teaching and scholarship. In striking contrast with this state of affairs, the recently issued document purporting to be the 'revised contract' of the tenured academics of at least one Irish university suggests that Irish Higher Education employers will be henceforth entitled to discipline and dismiss academics for not cooperating with their employer's 'plans, goals and objectives'. It further requires that academics seek their employers' written permission for 'external activities' (writing a book like this one?) that might damage the 'university's interests'.

To the unsuspecting, the addition of a loyalty clause to the academic contract could appear perfectly reasonable. And it would be reasonable if, but only if, the 'plans, goals and objectives' of all Irish universities could be relied upon to serve the worthiest of Higher Education imperatives. As we will see, however, much available evidence points to the fact that some, if not many, universities are actively promoting the kinds of short-term commercial aims and objectives that all too often militate against academic concerns and educational priorities. If destructive moves – like the downgrading of certain 'critical' subjects – were being made well before the Irish economy crashed, how much more likely are they to proliferate in hopeless budgetary situations? We can perhaps expect other Irish universities to follow the example of the one that announced to staff in 2010 that the only academics who would henceforth be recognised as worthy of preferment would be those bringing in non-exchequer funding. This latter policy might even extend, as it did recently in the University of Birmingham, to threatening to punish – that is, to 'fine' – those conscientious academic units which turn down applications from lucrative overseas students, no matter how poorly qualified the latter might be, linguistically for example. Furthermore, if the values and standards of Higher Education are being driven south because of funding pressures, then it stands to reason that university managers are going to have to find ways of neutralising any intellectual opposition that might be forthcoming. The only way of doing this is to weaken the culture of intellectual freedom, if necessary by rewriting the academic contract or by reducing the number of academics with security of contract. In the US, not only is the ratio of tenured academics to contingent, temporary or 'non-tenured' staff about 3:7, but 30 to 40 per cent of instructors are not just temporary staff but also part-time. These are the most vulnerable of all and the most poorly paid; 'piece-workers' without prospects, they can be pushed around the chess board at will. The situation is still much better in Ireland, at least as far as posts involving both teaching and research are concerned. Where the two are de-coupled, however, the situation of 'pure' researchers or of 'pure' teachers will inevitably be more precarious.

The dangers associated with the undermining of the academic profession need no further underlining for now. Chief amongst them is the fuelling of a vicious circle whereby, in the absence of the critical freedom associated with security of academic survival, educational standards continue to fall.

HIGHER EDUCATION: FOR WHAT?

To ask what Higher Education is for is a little like asking what life or humanity is for. Perhaps, though, the most commonly agreed function of Higher Education right across the world is, as Ellen Schrecker notes, to supply governments with an 'ideological buffer against demands from [the] underprivileged' for a more equal distribution of the nation's wealth.

> [A] college education is central to the American Dream. It offers the main – and often the only – assurance of economic advancement for most men and women without athletic ability or musical talent.

The same could probably be said today of the 'Irish Dream'. In Ireland too 'a college degree' is still regarded as the principal if not the only prospect of social ascent and economic prosperity for the young.

There are, however, a number of obvious problems associated with this strictly utilitarian view of education in terms of economic exchange. First, there is the unavoidable question of the relation between the economic cost and price of a 'college degree', on the one hand, and its buying power, on the other. Is a college degree really going to be a guarantee of employment, prosperity and social mobility in the new economic dis-order? The answer is – if not highly uncertain – then at least highly variable depending on the discipline and the particular 'college brand'. In her courageous book *Does Education Matter? Myths about Education and Economic Growth*, the London-based educationalist Alison Wolf questions the received wisdom that more investment in Higher Education necessarily increases economic growth. Wolf argues that what really makes a difference to the buoyancy of an economy are the mathematical and linguistic skills learned at school.

Then there is the problem of the link between the intrinsic value of Higher Education and the exchange value of certification or qualification. Alison Wolf challenges the logic that requires a Higher Education qualification to operate a cappuccino machine.

And finally there is the question of the link between a university education and civic or social benefit. Ellen Schrecker's book does, of course, recognise that Higher Education confers not just economic, but also non-material social or civic benefit:

> The academy protects the American mind. In a world of sound bites and bullet points, the nation's campuses are among the last few places where it is still possible to deal with complicated ideas or entertain orthodox opinions. Professors are the nation's main public intellectuals; they raise the questions with which an informed citizenry must deal. They are, therefore, essential to the preservation of the reasoned debate and unfettered expression that our democratic system requires.

If, however, Higher Education is in danger of being prevented from upholding its civic and democratic function as a forum of 'reasoned debate and unfettered expression', then with all the questions hanging over its value as a sure-fire way of boosting the economy and as a guarantee of social mobility, what exactly is it going to be good for? Especially if, to cap everything, it sells out on what it has traditionally prided itself on protecting, namely, fully rigorous intellectual endeavour?

HIGHER EDUCATION: FOR WHOM?

The first concern of any educationalist has to be access to the best possible education for all humankind. What the Irish public has no doubt understood as being the two fundamental challenges facing Irish Higher Education are funding and access, since these are the only two issues regularly highlighted in the media. Certainly, these are urgent and important questions. Yet we risk coming up with the wrong answers to them if we ignore a third matter, which is the value or purpose of Higher Education.

What do the principles of an academic Higher Education system for all, of infinitely elastic admissions and throughput targets, mean in practice? What happens, for example, if graduation or retention objectives targets force academics to set the bar ever lower in order to ensure that throughput objectives are reached? Will this not result in a perversion, or a disintegration, of academic standards? And what if the entire system starts to work to an inflationary certification model rather than to an educational one? If it is guided principally by commercial values, constraints or targets, rather than by educational imperatives, who really loses out? The most academically hungry students, fed see-through gruel instead of proper mind food? The less academic students, square pegs forced to contort themselves into miserable shapes and never allowed to know the truth about their standard of attainment? Or society as a whole, which needs deeply academic minds, certainly, but also artistic, spiritual, practical, intuitive and wildly innovative minds, not to mention people whose particular talent or skill is not academic or theoretical, but practical, manual, sporting, spiritual, nurturing, healing and so on.

It is clear that from Tibet to Pakistan, from Russia to Malawi and Japan to Haiti, we live in an imperfect world with unequal distribution of all sorts of goods, including education. Furthermore, systematic, large-scale and extreme human efforts to effect a more equitable redistribution have been, so far, unsuccessful or catastrophic. Now we are trying capitalism for all and trusting that markets will iron everything out globally. Historically, systems of Higher Education have always served the dominant ideology. Whether that was theological, feudal, communist, capitalist, liberal or neoliberal, universities mirrored it. Certainly, in the currently dominant high-capitalist system of globalisation, real efforts have been made to bridge the gap between educational birthright and financial or cultural means. In fairness, many if not most Eastern and Western, Northern and Southern states, along with supra-state agencies like the World

Bank or the OECD, have worked with individual state education systems on developing access programmes based on meritocratic policies. However, all the access, meritocratic or redistributive programmes in the world will not ensure that the core principles and standards of education are upheld once the academy has internalised the multiple pressures tending in a different direction towards unrestrained consumerism. In order for that line to be held, reverse pressure must be forthcoming from strong and united forces determined to defend the intrinsic value of education. In other words, teachers, students and parents, and society at large, would all have to share a prevailing, life-enhancing understanding of what Higher Education is for, if we are to rescue it from the death wish that is currently submerging its integrity.

ACADEMIC MONOPOLY: WHOSE LOSS?

In one way, in Ireland as elsewhere, academic values are victims of the monopoly of a fundamentally pseudo-academic industry. It is more or less assumed that the vast majority of secondary-school leavers will 'go to college' to continue their (so-called academic) education at a higher level. In Ireland specifically, an apparently unquestioning emphasis is placed on a largely and even exclusively academic trajectory as the model for one and all. All the talk is about the 'knowledge' economy, and when skills are mentioned, it is automatically assumed that these skills are technological, scientific, intellectual. In other words, it is taken for granted that all knowledge is 'academic' knowledge. If the secondary school system essentially and more or less exclusively grooms students for further academic study, what does that say to those who are not academically keen? What does it say about how society values the contribution that they will make? What does it say to those who, academically keen or not, might have both the talent and the desire to be painters or cabinetmakers, musicians or athletes, cooks or electricians, stonemasons or homemakers? With some notable exceptions, which the public rarely if ever hears about, Irish society seems to be fixated on a one-size-fits-all view of (so-called) academic achievement, seeing it as the means (for all) to one single end, or worse, as the means to another means, to another means, and so on and on and on. And sometimes, for those who struggle even more than for those who coast, it's fulfilment all the way. But if the mind is not being fed real food it's just an empty and exhausting ordeal for the student. And if minimal standards of rigour are not being set and adhered to, it's a swindle.

Empty ordeal or not, swindle or not, students who do a first academic diploma or degree at college or university will usually find that it is not enough. Fourth level being the new third level, they will find that they need to acquire ever more qualifications. Indeed, in its questionable wisdom, EU bureaucracy via the Bologna process has standardised Higher Education into a 3 + 2 structure (a three-year licenciate followed by a two-year masters degree). Increasingly, students will find that, while the three-year primary degree leads nowhere much, society will eventually start to scratch its head about all that extra time spent acquiring a Masters degree. For, as we will see, the trend in third and even fourth level education is for graduates to emerge – even from the 'top' colleges – superlatively qualified yet fundamentally (some even in their own eyes, but many quite obliviously) 'under-educated'. To put it more plainly, some, perhaps many, of these supposed 'masters' of their subjects are emerging as academic virgins, never having experienced, not even once, the hit of total absorption in the study of some academic subject or topic as an end in itself.

The uncritical and inflationary promotion of so-called academic credit as the be-all and end-all of youthful life and meaning is part of the battlefront on which (truly) academic values have been de-natured. The hype and the mania surrounding the manner in which Irish students are fed from second level into third level pseudo-academic pipelines is probably not limited to the Leaving Certificate; no doubt it affects the baccalaureate, the Abitur, A-Levels and SATs also. However, for sheer reductiveness it is hard to beat the premises of the *Irish Times* school league tables, which rank schools exclusively as feeding funnels for third-level education. These tables implicitly reduce the value of the education provided in the various schools by boiling it down to the proportion of students who proceed to register for 'high point' college courses. It must, however, be clear to all that neither the latter, nor even the very 'highest point' courses, are necessarily the courses that either require or foster the most able or incisive intellects, and they are certainly not the courses guaranteed to attract the most creative or independent spirits either. Quite to the contrary in some cases, probably. Apart entirely, then, from its exposure of the greasy but age-old correspondence between the most highly-fenced courses, the most lucrative professions and the most expensive private preparatory or grind-schooling, this yearly mis-identification and mis-evaluation of genuine educational value is deeply dispiriting.

Although it extends far beyond my competence, it is impossible to ignore here the question of an alternative to the over-valued, over-promoted, exclusively but not always genuinely academic, and sometimes downright phoney, Higher Education trajectory for all. Perhaps there is no viable alternative. Or perhaps the German 'dual system' of apprenticeship offers a healthier educational approach to skills that are not exclusively, not principally, or perhaps not at all academic. Not least because many if not most of these skills are actually impossible to de-localise to cheap-labour economies or to replace by artificial intelligence. Several factors recommend this vocational approach (which is or was applied elsewhere too – for example, Switzerland and Australia). Consider first of all the number and diversity of skills catered for, all of which are scrupulously regulated by the dual system which keeps apprentices involved in formal education for 20-30 per cent of their time and strictly regulates

65

the parameters of their on-the-job training (there are 342 *Ausbil-dungsberufe* or recognised occupations). Secondly, consider the level of German professionalism and craftwork and the social respect that it commands. Thirdly, note the fact that Germany's youth unemployment rates are the lowest in Europe. Whatever the hidden flaws of this system, the contrast is striking with the levels of corrosively misplaced prestige attaching (in the Irish system for one) to exclusively academic qualifications, however inflated or mediocre. In 2003, between 50 and 60 per cent of all young Germans under the age of 22 completed an apprenticeship, sometimes before proceeding to undertake more 'academic' studies. In that same year, one in three German companies offered apprenticeships and the following year the government signed an agreement with the trade unions which stipulates that all companies except very small ones must be willing to take on apprentices.

The author Paulo Coelho wrote about the cultural monopoly of academia in *Like the Flowing River: Thoughts and Reflections* (2005):

> Most of my friends, and most of my friends' children also, have degrees. That doesn't mean that they've managed to find the kind of work they wanted. Not at all. They went to university because someone, at a time when universities were important, said that, in order to rise in the world, you had to have a degree. And thus the world was deprived of some excellent gardeners, bakers, antique dealers, sculptors, and writers. Perhaps this is the moment to review the situation. Doctors, engineers, scientists, and lawyers need to go to university, but does everyone?

Coelho's provocative view that universities are only good for offering professional qualification and training clashes of course with the fact that a third of Irish Higher Education provision is in the arts and humanities. It also clashes with the widely recognised likelihood that it is impossible to predict exactly which strengths and skills will be required ten years hence. His unsettling purpose is no doubt to force his readers to think about what exactly it is that our society expects of a university or a college degree: image or substance, a mere qualification, an employment voucher, or the fulfilment of a real education?

Meanwhile, as this book goes to press, Ireland appears to be in the grip of near hysteria concerning, for example, criteria of entry to college and secondary education as a preparation for entry to Higher Education. That hysteria suggests strongly that we have no collective internal compass for finding true north, educationally speaking. Perhaps the first step to take in orientating ourselves is to ask which values exactly do we want Irish Higher Education to represent and defend.

ACADEMIC STANDARDS? EDUCATIONAL CONTINUUM AND CONTAGION

The way in which Irish students are educated at second level is of course related to the core concerns of this book. However, the focus here is on what ensues after they have emerged from the points race and the grind schools, following years of gaming the exam system via question prediction, honing exam technique, and so on. The problem is that by that point it may be too late to correct a short life-time of educational distortion. In nearly three decades of teaching at third level, I would have to accept that there has been a definite decline in general levels of academic attainment both at entry and at exit. The most academically gifted and motivated students are probably comparable from one year or decade to the next, but for the others, the bar has been progressively lowered beyond recognition. Certainly, greater self-confidence has made undergraduates more forthcoming over the past decade or so, and this factor, added to greater demographic diversity generally, makes for rewarding class contact. Unfortunately, however, if students come to college with a poor level of basic academic attainment, a low level of literacy for example (little sense of the structure of language – grammar or syntax and an inability to analyse, recognise or organise ideas), even strenuous remediation may not suffice to correct it. Increasingly, despite all the remedial writing and numeracy clinics made available to undergraduates in Irish (and presumably other) universities, and despite the 'modules in study-skills' offered to, or imposed upon, first-year students in some 'top' Irish universities, the academic slope is proving just too steep to climb. The issue is not so much that struggling students will 'drop out' or 'fail'. It is far more serious than that. A much more likely scenario is that many will emerge from university or college at more or less exactly the same point of educational attainment as that at which they entered, but furnished with an academic qualification, typically a respectable degree. And some may even proceed to teach at second level. This is where complete systems failure beckons.

When Irish university authorities claim that the secondary education system is not preparing students properly for Higher Education, they are probably right up to a point. But we need to remember that Irish universities bear more or less sole responsibility both for the academic education and the pedagogical training of teachers. That situation is changing since the private for-profit college Hibernia entered the teacher-training market to loudly favourable noises from the current coalition government. But certainly the academic standards, aspirations and principles of secondary education are largely determined by those prevailing in the public university and college sector. More broadly still, education is a continuous loop: what happens at one level or in one sector (commercialism and privatisation included) affects the whole secondary/tertiary and public/private continuum.

In many ways, the issues faced by both second and third level are exactly the same. There is, first and foremost, the fundamental social and political problem of privatisation and commercialisation. In his book *Global Education Inc.* (2012), Stephen Ball shows how all levels of education worldwide are being shaped by the interests of 'edu-businesses, neo-liberal advocacy networks and policy entrepreneurs'. Education policy is, in other words, being bought and sold as a profitable transnational commodity. Similarly, basic policy issues such as educational development, access and quality are being addressed almost exclusively through 'market solutions', by involving 'private providers' in the delivery of 'educational services', both independently and on behalf of the state. While himself avoiding a simplistic analysis, Ball paints a picture of globalised education in which 'universities, schools and education services are being acquired as assets by private equity companies'.

Although Stephen Ball remains fairly agnostic on its benefits and drawbacks, the privatisation of education – fuelled by what he calls the 'neo-liberal imaginary' – while it may not exacerbate it, is definitely not going to reverse academic Armageddon. It is not going to undo the disastrous decimation of the morale of the teaching profession and it is not going to counter the (probably associated) decline in standards of core academic attainment across levels and sectors. In Higher Education, this decline is simultaneously masked and exacerbated by rising number of graduates and by grade inflation. Given the contradiction between those trends (declining standards and rising outputs/outcomes), the higher grades and increased numbers of graduates can hardly be attributed to a better study ethic, to better teaching, to superior technology or to the accelerated evolution of human intelligence. Both second and third levels also suffer from the plague of almost exclusively credential- or assessment-directed learning. Furthermore, some of the solutions proposed to these problems have been tested in Higher Education and have proved less than satisfactory. Continuous or constant evaluation rather than terminal or summative assessment, project-work or team-work, and credit for non-academic participation are just some of the most obvious 'answers' which seem to cause as many problems as they solve. There are, of course, signs that educational policy-makers appreciate the importance of not throwing out the baby of essential groundwork with the bathwater of 'rote learning', and of holding the line concerning the value of education as an end in itself. Indeed, the current president of one of Ireland's largest and oldest universities is on record as wanting to hold that line in relation to college admissions policy. However, some of the less enlightened, so-called 'fixes' that have been proposed to date (for example, the extra testing intended to square the circle of medical school admissions) inspire little confidence in the abilities of those bodies responsible for steering or leading Irish Higher Education. The acid test to which all steering proposals must be put is, of course, their ability to re-focus education on deep understanding, on real, rigorous or precise thinking and on sustained attention to depth and to detail, rather than simply and solely on credits, grades and rankings.

ACADEMIC ARMAGEDDON: WHO CARES?

How is it that, although the Higher Education sector is expanding exponentially across the globe, certain core educational values and standards are on the run over the whole spectrum? Is it that some aspects of the commoditisation of education bleed it of legitimacy? In essence, the problem seems to be at its most acute where the university is most corporate, in other words, wherever the immediate commercial returns on research take priority, or wherever the student is treated as the customer and the academic as the employee of a service provider implicitly contracted to deliver sales targets and client satisfaction. In such a context, real education, not to mention *Higher* Education, can probably only take place to the extent that both students and academics find ways of circumventing or subverting that implicit contract.

One thing is certain, however: the haemorrhage of intrinsic academic principles from the meeting rooms and offices of

Higher Education, if not (yet) from the still-sacred space of the seminar-room, matters not just for a privileged few, an academic elite. Instead, the entire civic fabric of human society will be profoundly affected by any systematic de-meaning within Higher Education of intrinsic values and standards – that is, of anything that is not an immediate proxy for economic value. Wherever it opens up, the space of real education allows a deepening of thoughtfulness. And it encourages rigorous attention to complexity and detail. Regardless of the discipline studied, Higher Education is about that exacting and independent engagement with precision, profundity and complexity. Even the knowledge that such a space exists is important. Why? Because it affects the way whole societies think about being human.

2

The 'Global' Picture:
The Writing on the Wall
for Ireland

It is impossible to make sense of contemporary Irish Higher Education without recognising its microcosmic scale and its exceptional susceptibility to certain external influences. For many obvious reasons – historical, cultural and linguistic – the Irish corporate university has largely followed the US and UK models. This is why it is important to appreciate the scale of the academic subsidence currently being flagged within these bigger systems.

WORLD RANKINGS

The fact that Higher Education worldwide has been taken over by an overwhelming concern with international university rankings is both a symptom and a reinforcing factor of the corporate creep associated with globalisation. Even the most infatuated rankings fan would have to admit that there is something peculiar about universities from different countries and continents competing for places in universal league tables, despite extraordinary variations in sheer demographic scale, in historical evolution and in educational and linguistic culture. We only have to think of the disparities within university culture on the same continent: in England on the one hand, and France on the other, for example. In France, universities have traditionally played second fiddle to the Napoleonic inheritance of 'grandes écoles', those famous republican incubators of the French elites, like the *École Polytechnique* or the *École Nationale d'Administration*. However, even the French republican model is now wobbling under the combined pressure of a growing corporate orientation and a proliferation of private post-baccalaureate provision.

The clear implication of global rankings is that standardised criteria can and should be applied to all colleges and universities regardless of the specificity of their local context. However, just when we pride ourselves on living in a world 'gone global', and just when information has gone viral, when universities can podcast lectures and debates, in other words when people can have relatively cheap global access to commoditised 'knowledge' without paying exorbitant fees or without uprooting themselves, what are we doing? Paradoxically, we're locating educational excellence within the walls of individual institutions and we're accepting corresponding increases in competition and pricing for this proprietary or branded product. In other words, humungous prices are being paid for the particular 'college experience', the particular facilities and the particular clientele attracted by a particular brand. What this suggests is that, although it is becoming ever more feasible to transmit knowledge and 'know-how' in real time, at little expense and across great distances, education is still 'being sold', at the top at least, as having everything to do with 'being there', in a specific place, and indeed as everything to do with 'being there with (certain) others'. There is, of course, some truth and merit in this approach. But two caveats apply. One concerns access, the other standards. These concerns are related. Wherever access is restricted – either through selection or pricing – the risk of closed-shop 'group-think' arises. And thereby the risk of a fall in real or independent thinking. There is no doubt that 'being there with others' and 'learning from peers' are indeed essential and critical to a (truly) Higher Education. Indeed, the biggest single difference in the educational level or standard of universities – or, for that matter, of second-level schools – is probably made by relative levels of authentic – that is, truly academic – peer input and aspiration. Although the 'very top' US universities like Harvard may seem to have reached this nirvana, we will see that the money-power-knowledge nexus in which they are embedded is at best problematic. And this is why the aspirations of certain private, would-be Harvards – such as London's 'New College for the Humanities' – are also fundamentally flawed.

It is equally problematic, however, to abolish academic selection by dropping standards to the point of pretending that we can, with impunity, take the calculus out of Maths or the grammar out of language. Although a diversity of student backgrounds is normally a plus, education cannot happen without active critical engagement on all of the students' parts. Furthermore, although equality of opportunity is an essential principle of social democracy, any opening of access that involves dropping real academic standards will never, ever square the Higher Education circle. Why not? Because for Higher Education to happen, it is surely important, but it is not enough, to gain access and to attend. All *real* students bring grounding and aptitude as well as engagement to the table. Furthermore, truly 'Higher' education is more likely to happen not online, nor through the monologue of lectures, but in much more interactive settings. And for these to be effective, there must be not just co-location in real time and space, but also expert and dedicated moderation and small class sizes. All these factors make real Higher Education costly. But even then, if too many students in a given seminar lack the motivation, interest, understanding and ability to participate at a high enough level, then even small group teaching will not work.

This is why globally, as well as nationally, universities and colleges are in competition with each other both for the best researchers and for 'the best' students. When it is a question, as it often is, of course, of chasing genuine academic merit and motivation, such competitiveness is educationally legitimate. There are many reasons, however, to be profoundly sceptical about the ways in which recruitment competition plays out in practice. Interestingly, domestic rather than world league tables are the ones that really concern American universities (not that there is much difference between the two since US universities dominate the top 10 and the top 100 in the world rankings). Yet the fact is that some US public universities appear to have been almost bankrupted by the resources spent – or squandered – on countering national competition. In Ireland, we will only know with hindsight the degree of real and lasting benefit accruing to the national Higher Education system from the investments made by individual universities in seeking to gain a competitive advantage in the (national) numbers game or the (international) rankings race. Three things are clear, however. One, the Irish university consistently positioned highest in the world rankings is not the one that invested most resources in overt national competition, laying claim – for example – to the position of 'Ireland's education capital' or 'Ireland's premier university'. Another is that in and around the boom, appointments in Ireland to the most senior or 'trophy' Higher Education posts appear to have often involved, in some of the more unsubtly competitive universities at least, costly transfers from other Irish institutions. And finally, one of the most aggressive domestic student recruitment drives mounted in Irish Higher Education in recent years was demonstrably based on the application of a damaging educational gimmickry which will take years, if not decades, to flush out.

An Irish academic, Ellen Hazelkorn, has written a most accomplished critique of the basis of university league tables and there is no need for me to repeat her analysis here. One of her main concerns is that ranking competition is not, in fact, a tide that lifts all boats and that it actually deepens inequality. Other concerns would be that only about 5 per cent of the world's universities are reckoned to feature in any position at all in world league tables, and these all appear to be cloned on the corporate Anglo model. Despite such cautions, however, rankings are still massively regarded as an essential tool, not so much of informed consumer choice as of public education policy. So is this good or bad? Well, it depends on what we think Higher Education is for. If the aim is to make money out of it, then they are custom-built marketing vehicles (perhaps this is indeed their *raison d'être*). But if that is not the main aim, either for the individual or for society in general, then their basis and their effects are questionable.

If – suspending disbelief – we assume for a moment that there really is such a thing as the 'best university in the world', Harvard in 2010 or CalTech in 2011, followed by a list of the next best in a precise order of merit, right down to the 500th or 1000th, would this be a good or a bad thing? And for whom? Try as we might, it is actually very hard to suspend disbelief sufficiently to give these questions a serious answer. For one thing, even if it were possible to work out the exact criteria by which all universities everywhere should and could be measured, eventually and inevitably the differences between the top 500, top 1,000, top 10,000 universities would become ever more infinitesimal and the ranking ever more meaningless. However, even that first 'if' is a very big one, because it concerns the feasibility of measuring substantive or inherently meaningful value as opposed to an ever greater, but purely formal, convergence with exchange value. While it's perfectly feasible to measure exchange value, inherently meaningful value is another – far more complex and subjective – matter altogether. This is why the compilers of educational league tables have no option but to use proxies extensively in their definition of rank. These tables are supposed to measure various key performance indicators (another term for proxies) in order to establish a relative reputational order. In fact, however, they typically use reputational proxies tautologically as an indication of quality. Indeed some Irish university sources have blamed Irish Higher Education's 2011 slide down the world rankings on the perceived toxicity of Ireland's economic brand in general. Certainly, the kind of hearsay on which league tables are partly based involves asking, for example, the CEOs of major corporations to identify 'the best' universities worldwide. And one of the reasons why the Shanghai rankings were quickly out-ranked in plausibility by the *Times Higher Education* tables was that whereas the former re-lied on data provided by 15,000 self-selecting academics world-wide, the Times Higher Education (THE) survey collected data by invitation from its 13,000 academic informants. This adjust-ment, while welcome, does not completely answer the objection of circularity regarding both the selection of informants and the selection and weighting of various criteria.

Since the THE rankings have been 'powered' not, as before, by Quacquarelli Symonds (QS) but rather by the self-styled 'global information specialists' Thomson Reuters, the criteria have become somewhat more focussed on teaching (that is, on students). Teaching/Learning has been promoted from really poor relation to counting half as much as research. The problem is, though, that when proxies such as 'student retention' rates or 'time to completion' are regarded as valid indicators of the educational value of a given institution, there remains a major credibility deficit. For obvious reasons, poor retention rates in particular can sometimes be a sign of high rather than low ac-ademic standards, as indeed can the time given to students to complete projects.

The rule of rankings does have consequences. First of all, as ranked criteria exert ever more traction on university policy, there is a risk that measurable values will be the only ones that universities will invest in. Even if that means betraying other valid – but less easily quantifiable – principles. It would appear, indeed, that rankings offer perverse incentives to game the assessment process. Thus, if factors such as the international composition of the student and staff demographic are considered as indicators of excellence (this factor counts for 7.5 per cent of credit allowed by the THE rankings, with 60 per cent allowed for research, 30 per cent for teaching and 2.5 per cent for technology transfer), that's not so difficult to organise. Approximately 19 per cent of the student body of Ireland's largest university currently comprises international students, coincidentally exactly the same percentage as the current proportion of international students across the US Higher Education system. Indeed, that Irish university's stated aim is to 'grow' this figure right up to 30 per cent. How, though, is the fact of having a high proportion of overseas students a guarantee of a given university's greatness? Unless those students can be demonstrated to be pushing up academic standards on the programmes in question, the opposite could quite easily be the case – and if the students' linguistic skills or entry-level standard of education are below-par, for example, then it will inevitably be thus. But there again, if education systems are going to be ranked with reference to circular proxies and/or preponderantly on the basis of metrics that do not reliably value institutional ethos or governance, critical integrity, social or global justice, freedom of expression or freedom from exploitation, then educationalist hearts have plenty to bleed for before they shed a few less liberal drops for falling academic standards.

Even those with less haemophiliac hearts will readily appreciate the differential effect on academic standards of spectacularly wealthy and dramatically broke universities alike setting themselves identical international enrolment targets. Whereas the former can attract the world's most gifted students with postgraduate scholarship packages valued at close to six digits per annum, the latter are going to be counting on international tuition fee dowries, often for undergraduate degrees, to balance their books. Unfortunately, Irish Higher Education seems at risk of falling ever more deeply into this second, 'hustler' category and some institutions seem, as we will see, particularly reckless in respect of the possible reputational risks involved, risks already mentioned here as having been exposed in recent UK media reports. On 26 June 2012, for example, the *Daily Telegraph* sported a front-page headline: 'How foreign students with lower grades jump the university queue.' The article was based on an undercover investigation of the *modus operandi* of the major student recruitment agency used by British universities in China. The particular agent interviewed boasted of being able to open doors to under-qualified applicants in certain named UK universities. Then on July 5th the *Telegraph* ran an article headlined 'Foreign recruitment agents "paid £60m by universities"'. This article piggybacked on a *Times Higher Education* study that found that most of that money was paid by the universities on a commission basis (£1,000 per student recruited). Seven of the ten respondent universities couldn't say how much the agency charged the recruits themselves (presumably a lot!). The same study found, predictably, that some UK universities (Oxbridge, Imperial, LSE) do not use recruitment agencies at all. With universities everywhere so dependent on this income stream, however, there is little chance of overseas recruitment practices changing soon, despite the UK Education Minister's call for an investigation.

In some respects university rankings resemble the credit ratings currently used to tar and feather national economies in the global financial marketplace. The 2011 slide in the positions of Irish universities from the 2009 or 2010 picture can be looked at in this light. This sudden trend reversal, from climb to slide, was interpreted in diametrically different ways by various Irish interests: some university leaders saw it as proof of the intolerable impact of funding deficits, while public sector bashers seized it as ammunition to fire at the work-ethic of Irish academics. The most plausible explanation of the apparent fall is most unlikely, however, to be a sudden decision by Irish academics to slack off, much less super-sensitive year-on-year measurement of the impact of recent funding cutbacks (for example, the frozen budgets of some Irish university libraries, reduced library opening hours, larger class sizes, and so on). It is much more likely to reflect the fact that it is becoming ever more difficult to play the Higher Education rankings game to win. Ever more numerous universities, especially from 'emerging markets', are now jostling for places at the so-called top and even breaking into the top 100, for example, the University of Peking (to which Ireland's profitable Hibernia College formally announced its engagement at the end of the February 2012 trade visit to Ireland of China's Vice-President) and the National University of Singapore, recently wedded to Yale. Furthermore, the ascent of some of these rising international stars is undoubtedly favoured by their ability to shed some of the brakes on competitiveness hampering other players, such as the constraints linked to such old-fashioned social or democratic ideals as freedom of speech and assembly as well as more specific ideals such as critical independence, security of tenure, intellectual freedom and dignity in the academic workplace. This is the background against which we need to judge the real significance not just of ranking nosedives but also of magical levitations.

Another consequence of ranking syndrome is its reinforcement of a remarkably reductive cultural homogenisation across Higher Education systems. This is a particularly dramatic trend in a continent like Europe where cultural and linguistic diversity has been so positively valued historically, and where the balance between more universalist or federative, and more particularist or separatist ideals is one of continuing and, if anything, growing sensitivity. For example, in an age of putative global convergence, our continent now numbers sixteen states more than it did in 1988. Yet how many universities operating and promoting work in languages other than 'Globish' are going to be valued as such in our global future? And will this trend towards Globish convergence not necessarily undermine or obliterate the importance, world wide, of disciplines that study or value cultural and linguistic difference? Although ranking designers are working on the problem, the toxicity of global league tables towards cultural and linguistic diversity is probably intractable.

It is true, of course, that cultural diversity does not have an automatically positive value, especially when repressive political regimes hide behind nationalism, sectarianism, or cultural relativism to deny certain citizens (children, women, ethnic minorities...) their full civic and human rights. Innumerable universities worldwide are currently facing down threats of this kind, which do not always emanate from repressive state authorities. At the University of Manouba near Tunis, for example, as oppositional fundamentalist (Salafist) groups engaged in open conflict with secular and progressive interests in the spring of 2012, acute concerns were caused by an open Salafist violation of the national Tunisian flag flying on campus. And, again in the spring of 2012, at the Medical and Pharmacy University of Tirgu Mures in Romania, extremist Hungarian nationalist elements were trying to insist that the one-third minority of expatriate Hungarian students be instructed in Hungarian apart from their Romanian peers. Perhaps the roots of sectarian fundamentalism will be weakened over time by the obvious benefits accruing to the citizens of either threatened or repressive states from the increased external openings and flows of Higher Education. If so, it will be the major good news story emerging from the internationalisation of Higher Education. For now, however, Higher Education's globalisation agenda is not at all focused on the often uphill struggle to democratise and universalise a genuinely liberating educational ideal. All too often, the internationalisation/globalisation agenda is not at all engaged in challenging the forces of political darkness at work in the wider world of Higher Education. Instead, the narrow sights of so-called 'global' universities are to all appearances largely and resolutely trained, in Ireland as elsewhere as we will see, on circular commercial ends.

KNEE-JERK GLOBALISM

The globalisation of the Higher Education market involves the same pitfalls and mirages as the globalisation of all other markets, but it poses particular problems also. First of all, it is an overwhelmingly Globish-speaking phenomenon. For this linguistic reason and others, the phenomenon that we call 'globalisation' actually excludes vast swathes of the globe in its pretensions to world-wide reach. In other words, the supposedly 'globalised' world leaves out much, if not most, of the global population, that is, it excludes most of South and Central America as well as Africa, Russia and quite a lot of India and Europe too. In fact, the 'globish' Higher Education consensus is modelled on the so-called but now defunct 'Washington consensus', itself centred on subservience to market forces and to the policy of market liberalisation long favoured by the World Bank and the IMF. This explains why ranking fever – to which even the traditionally idiosyncratic, but in many ways admirable, French educational system seems to be gradually falling victim too – brings with it a hollow and mimetic 'global' formatting. As universities which send business or science students to study in France well know, it can be difficult to persuade French universities to teach them through French, partly because the French themselves feel that their own language is somehow not sufficiently 'globish'. Similarly, mid-2012, the Technological University of Milan announced that all of its graduate courses are to be delivered henceforth not in Italian, but in English. All over the world, 'wannabe global' universities are trying to enhance their transnational competitiveness. University College London has had a new tag-line emblazoned over its Gower Street entrance: 'London's Global University'. The University of Singapore calls itself 'South-East Asia's Global University'. And Ireland's UCD, having opened a 'Global Ireland Institute' in

2008, the following year launched a new strategic plan with the grandiose title of 'Forming Global Minds'.

The increased international dimension of Higher Education is something to be celebrated; of that there is no doubt. This opening has deepened and transformed the educational experience of students right across the whole world. The immensely successful Erasmus and Erasmus Mundus programmes are a case in point. However, whereas the ethos of such genuine international exchange and mobility projects is based on respect for cultural difference and for cross-cultural understanding, the 'global' agenda is quite different. Certainly, cross-cultural enrichment and international understanding may be a serendipitous by-product of the global re-formatting to which corporate universities aspire. But in general, as with the imperial or colonial agenda, the global agenda is primarily commercial. Nobody who reads the measured caveats of the American educationalist Philip Altbach about the pitfalls of the global agenda currently dominating the 'internationalisation' strategies of universities worldwide will fail to be convinced that we may well be looking here at a gigantic speculative bubble. Altbach is professor of Higher Education and director of the Centre for International Higher Education at Boston College. Commenting on the vogue for universities establishing 'branches' and collaborations overseas, especially in Asia and in the Gulf, he recalls the fact that of the twenty or so branches of American universities established in Japan in the 1980s, just two survived. Perhaps those expanding universities made a nett killing in Japan, perhaps they didn't. But unless they were looking after educational standards at home, the investment won't have been their greatest hour.

BRANDING CONSENSUS: THE WASHINGTON ADVISORY GROUP

Over more than a decade, many Irish universities, whose sights were trained on the global league, called on the services of a private US consultancy firm called the Washington Advisory Group. The list of university clients currently advertised online by this consultancy includes very few international names, and strictly no French, German or British universities. Of the seven international universities named as clients, one is in Saudi Arabia, one in India, one in Turkey and *four* in Ireland. At the time when (at least) four Irish universities (TCD, UCD, UL and DCU) called on its services, it was an LECG–owned private research and education management consultancy. It boasted the services of, amongst other US luminaries, retired university presidents and corporate technocrats. LECG went into liquidation in April 2011, almost a year after the WAG's grey matter had withdrawn to a different NASDAQ-cited consortium called Huron, which seems to specialise in what must be that sector's equivalent of ambulance chasing (bankruptcy, liquidation, insolvency steering etc.). In Huron, the re-named 'Advisory Group' has jettisoned the W-word with its echoes of the erstwhile supreme but now disgraced 'Washington consensus'. This team of management consultants specialises, just as it did when it was still the WAG, in providing blueprints for national and global success to public and private universities, but most especially medical schools and institutes. It also advises other research-intensive organisations. Its speciality is the provision of master classes in Higher Education and research branding with a particular emphais on medical science. The group's lookalike reports are available for perusal on the internet. One of the more telling is the May 2010 report delivered to (another) UCD, the University of California at Davis. The Group appears to have a number of blind spots. Certainly, it seems rather out of its depth in relation to place or context. Europe seems to be for it a wholly 'foreign country'. Far more importantly, the Group seems consistently short on insights into the humanities and, even worse, into undergraduate studies across the board. In fact, its reports typically make little or no mention of students and even less of undergraduate students. A rather exclusive emphasis on research strategising is in fact the most reliable sign of its neo-con, high-capitalist footprint. Its reports on domestic universities were/are essentially recipes for 'leveraging' more funding by moving up into the next league of national peers, both on a discipline-by-discipline basis and on an institution-wide basis. One piece of homespun advice to UC Davis was to send a mole/lobbyist to park him/herself full-time in Washington DC, presumably as close as possible to the West Wing. Internationally, the key footprint of this consultancy, wherever it has passed, is a recommendation for university re-form, always centred on the same handful of corporate strategies and structures, and all stamped with the Group's by now ageing motto: 'global or bust'.

Public and Private Models: The US, UK and Us

For decades, universities everywhere, including the UK but par-ticularly perhaps in Ireland – the WAG's star international pupil after all – have been mesmerised by the US. The USA has been, in other words, the global trendsetter. In a most arresting article in the *Times Higher Education*, 'A Weather Eye on the US Storm' (February 2011), Sarah Cunnane confirms that the US Higher Education system is typically held up as a model of world-class excellence for the rest of the world. 'At first glance,' she adds, 'this seems entirely fair.' After all, US institutions dominated the *Times Higher Education* rankings in 2010, with 72 institutions in the top 100 and seven in the top ten alone. In the 2011 THE rankings, US universities number seven of the top ten (the other three being Oxbridge and Imperial College London).

Just as the notion of global-market competition is intimately linked to the US and indeed to Americanisation, so too the con-temporary notion of the 'research university' ('invented' by the German philosopher Wilhelm von Humboldt) was epitomised in the second half of the twentieth century by the most prestigious US universities. Unfortunately, however, the current model of the research-intensive corporate university is largely driven by the income-generation value of research. It is because of this, indeed, that the 'research university' has become a byword, primarily in the US itself, for a drift away from core educational purpose. In the US this commercialist drift is being regarded in certain circles not just as a threat to the traditional value of specifically academic, as opposed to industrial, research, but also as contributing to a deterioration of the standards of undergraduate education.

It is at this point that we need to look more closely at the specificity of US Higher Education and more especially at the principal differences between the UK and the US systems. One of the most important things to know about the US paradigm is that the majority of the 'top-ranked' US universities and colleges are private, even though there are also many public universities, such as UC Berkeley, which are equally prestigious. The public funding from which US public universities benefit is state-based rather than federal. Thus when the state of California went bankrupt, the University of California was in serious trouble. The private sector includes the Ivy League universities, which – a bit like the Irish pale – are concentrated in the Eastern US cradle of WASP privilege. Although still associated with the reproduction of class privilege, the top private universities and colleges, which typically charge far, far higher tuition fees than the public institutions, have greatly expanded their meritocratic dimension. And although these private institutions have also been hit by the economic crisis, their (substantial) endowments still provide them with something of a cushion. Conversely, the current funding situation of US public universities is in many cases very problematic and even critical at present.

In contrast to the US system, UK universities are almost exclusively public. However, in the face of Britain's recessionary economic situation many of them are now charging tuition fees which are higher than those charged even by the more expensive public universities in the US. To simplify somewhat, the current situation in the UK (excluding Scotland) is that the government has switched from subsidising universities to having private citizens incur significant debt to pay for their own or their children's education. The consequences are set to be very serious, not just for the future debtors, but also for certain disciplines, since students will inevitably have to shun any disciplines not promising the kinds of financial return likely to enable graduates to repay their tuition loans.

The other big difference between the two systems is a cultural one. Traditionally, although this is now beginning to change, US universities, including public or state institutions, enjoyed considerable autonomy. Conversely, in the post-Thatcher UK, and perhaps as a consequence of UK universities' dependence on central or national funding, standardised evaluation of the activities of British universities has been extraordinarily tight and intrusive. This supervision is modelled on what used to be called 'new public management', a system that (cl)aimed to translate the efficiency processes of private enterprise onto public institutions and services. It is based, broadly speaking, on audit-linked funding, itself implemented through management systems dominated by 'key performance indicators'. Oxford and Cambridge resisted this control very successfully, as did certain London universities, at least for a time. However, growing reactions, such as *What Are Universities For?* by Oxford academic Stefan Collini (2012) suggest that the centralised managerialist stranglehold and the commercial vice-grip are now compressing the independence of those institutions too. Moreover, the US fiscal crisis means that the suffocating grip of managerialism has now spread over the strained public university system in the US as well.

PRICING HIGHER EDUCATION: FOLLOWING THE US INTO THE WALL?

As tuition fees (even at public universities) and student debt soar in the US, there are calls for the UK sector to take note of

the distress signals emanating from the 'world's academic pow-
erhouse'. In an effort to point up the importance for the UK of
learning from US mistakes, Roger Brown, co-director of the
Centre of Higher Education Research Development at Liverpool
Hope University in the UK, who has already been referred to as
questioning the value of international rankings, produced a discussion paper entitled 'Lessons from America?' For Brown:

> There are striking parallels between the policies of in-
> creased competition . . . and reduced public funding . . .
> which are the central thrust of the Coalition Govern-
> ment's higher education policies, and the developments
> that have produced the current US system. Similar conse-
> quences may be anticipated.

In her *THE* article on the subject, Sarah Cunnane also quotes
Linda Cox Maguire, vice-chair of US consultancy firm Maguire
Associates, which advises higher education institutions in North
America.

> [T]he UK is in a very similar position to where the US was
> around 15 years ago and that's why it's so interesting for
> us to watch it. We've seen the storm on the horizon for
> the UK, and there's so much that can be learned from
> mistakes and successes we've had in the US.

According to the most recent figures, student tuition fees
in the US cover about 50 per cent of the total average cost of
educating undergraduates. Because of the emphasis on campus life, universities usually quote fee packages that include tuition, room and board. In 2008-09, the average undergraduate
fee package was estimated at $12,283 (public institutions) and
$31,233 (private). Over the previous ten years, costs had risen by
32 per cent at public institutions and 24 per cent at private institutions, even when adjusted for inflation. According to the most
recently available figures, 100 US institutions now charge more

than $50,000 a year (tuition fees plus room and board). Cunnane reports that:

> Mark C. Taylor, chair of the department of religion at Columbia University, has estimated that if current trends continue, the cost of a degree at a leading US institution could reach $330,000 by 2020.

In fact, Taylor argues that 'the most difficult aspect of the problems in American higher education has become the financial [one]' and that 'the economic model of higher education in the US is unsustainable'. To illustrate the credibility of this claim, Cunnane refers to the issue of student debt.

> [S]tudent debt is already of great concern in the US; in August 2010, a report was published showing that for the first time, debt from student loans had surpassed the nation's credit card debt.

However, sometimes universities find that even fee increases are not sufficient to stave off the ultimate catastrophe.

> [In early 2011] the University of Nevada, Las Vegas announced to staff that managers would be taking the first steps towards declaring financial exigency in response to a possible $47.5 million shortfall, revealed in the proposed budget of the state of Nevada. Exigency . . . is the term used for the declaration of bankruptcy for an academic institution. To begin with, though, the president of UNLV was looking at the possible 'elimination or condensation of colleges and schools . . . along with departmental eliminations and reorganisations'.

The stock university responses to credit crunches, apart from raising tuition fees, consist in freezing the hiring of academic staff, imposing increased teaching loads and bigger classes on existing staff, increasing the proportion of adjunct or temporary academic staff, deferring promotions, but also cutting programmes, merging disciplines and encouraging early retirements. Not only have similar austerity measures been applied in Irish Higher Education since 2008, but in certain (reforming or reformed) institutions many – particularly programme-pruning, staff cuts and discipline mergers – were applied to the least cherished (that is, least profitable) disciplines several years before the Irish boom crash-landed.

Surely the US and UK funding and student-debt crises are warning signs that Ireland cannot ignore? The main idea behind the current UK policy paper, the Browne Report, is that the full unleashing of market forces would lead to greater Higher Education competitiveness in terms of pricing and quality. What has happened, though, is that British universities have been allowed to increase tuition charges very sharply (again, the situation in Scotland is quite different, since Scottish students do not pay tuition fees at Scottish universities). Although, originally, only the very top UK universities were to charge top fees, the list of institutions opting to charge the £9,000 maximum steadily lengthened. So much for market forces driving down prices. And as for the expectation that they would push up standards, if we take it that private institutions are the ones most aligned on market forces, then contagion from the US for-profit sector bodes ill for that hope too. For example, Global Apollo, the American education-for-profit company that owns both the University of Phoenix in the US and the UK's BPP University College (whose university status dates only from 2010), was recently found by the US Higher Learning Commission to have misled students about the value of the qualifications offered. The same company lost an appeal against a US Supreme Court ruling that it had defrauded its shareholders by suppressing a Department of Education report critical of its standards. Of course, BPP points to its regulation by the UK Quality Assurance Agency. But, given the kinds of accreditation that slipped past that body before eventually being picked up – including a series of very dodgy University of Wales validations (described by the Wales education minister Leighton Andrews as 'bringing the brand of Wales into disrepute') – this is not watertight reassurance.

LESSONS FROM AMERICA: LOSING SIGHT OF THE POINT

In a circular logic, what some might regard as a simple side effect of the US universities' funding crisis could equally be regarded as one of the main causes of that crisis, namely, a drift away from a focus on education per se, replaced by a competitive fixation on research and revenue. Sarah Cunnane's THE article quotes Columbia University's Mark Taylor again in this connection:

> [A]s US universities raised fees over the past couple of decades, what we've found is that they became more and more focused on their own institutional needs and institutional missions and less on broader societal needs.

Cunnane also quotes Tom Palaima, professor of Classics at the University of Texas at Austin, who argues that a branding focus explains the 'large and often wasteful' expenditure on endeavours such as sports. Although sport expenditure does not really affect the UK or Irish Higher Education systems, Palaima argues that the UK should be wary of 'US institutions' preoccupation with building a brand.' For Columbia's Mark Taylor, it is above all an 'insane sense of ranking' that has caused many (US) universities to lose their focus on what matters in a manner disastrous for their finances. 'Everybody's trying to be number one all the time,' he complains.

> Some institutions borrowed far too much money and in the 1990s went on a building spree to try to attract students. They didn't build classrooms, they built fancy dorms and recreational sports facilities instead, and now their assets are down because the market has collapsed and these institutions are carrying a lot of debt.

To quote from an interview in *The Californian* with the writer Walter Kirn, who will have the last word in this second section of the book, the splendour of the 'massive edifices' sprouted by his alma mater, Princeton, contradicts the university's core mission:

> [T]here are still the same number of students, and the basic mission is still the same, which is to get them to read some good books, and I'm a little appalled by the outsized nature of Princeton's physical plant compared to the . . . ongoing nature of its academic mission, which is at somewhat the same level. These places remind me of modern cathedrals that donors would build wings on hoping they'd go to heaven. They're getting larger and larger, but their presence in society and the virtue that they're adding to our society has not grown in proportion.

As they tried to come to terms with the implications of spectacular tuition fee increases across the board, British Higher Education circles were thrown into uproar in 2011 by the announcement that a new, private and for-profit college, the 'New College of the Humanities' aka 'Grayling's Folly' (after its chief founder), was due to open for business in London in 2012-13 and was set to charge its undergraduates £18,000 annual tuition fees. Apart from the price tag, its piggy-back accreditation arrangement with the University of London has caused major controversy. Another cause for concern was the employment status of many of the star academics referred to on the college's website as the 'professoriate': some of these academics seemed to hold permanent appointments elsewhere, in the UK or in the US. At first blush, this initiative appeared to be a spoof, perhaps aiming to hold up a magnifying mirror to the all too real UK fee increases that are bound to put a university education, in certain disciplines anyway, beyond the reach of so many. But then came the details that confirmed that Professor Grayling and his co-founders were serious: for example, details about the equity funding behind the venture or about the founders' hopes to offer means-tested scholarships giving partial fee remission to up to 30 per cent of the student intake. The most ironic part of this story is the fact that the pre-advertised courses included 'critical thinking' and 'applied ethics'; indeed Dr Grayling himself is best-known as a philosopher of ethics. Although the 'New College' project is in many respects admirably upfront about its business plan, this openness merely amplifies the contradiction that it shares with any university engulfed by market priorities: namely, the lethal incompatibility between the means of imparting certain values, and the values themselves.

R&D, Innovation and Higher Education Labour

For Cary Nelson, former chair of the American Association of University Professors, the chief problem for American Higher Education is its 'increasing reliance on contingent labour'. Nelson blames the collapse of state budgets from 2002 to 2004 for the 'increased reliance on part-time and non-tenure track instruction'. The reason why this trend is so serious is because Higher Education is based on the symbiotic relation between educating students on the one hand, and commitment to academic research or scholarship on the other. While some academics might be more passionate about either their own research/scholarship or about teaching, those who devote themselves exclusively to one or the other activity should surely be the exception rather than the rule.

In his book *The University: An Owner's Manual* (1991), the academic economist Henry Rosovsky, former Dean of the Faculty of Arts and Sciences at Harvard, vaunts the value for students of attending a research university as opposed to a strictly pedagogically-oriented institution. Rosovky's uncontroversial definition of research is 'studious inquiry, usually critical and exhaustive investigation of experimentation having for its aim the revision of accepted conclusions in the light of newly discovered facts'. He claims that research-oriented teaching staff will be more likely to entertain an optimistic belief in progress and less likely to be world-wearily cynical or to suffer from the burnout that comes from teaching the same things over and over. Although this seems to be a rather condescending view of the teaching vocation, it is probably true that the perennially curious and studious academic with an exhaustively critical and creative approach to their subject makes for an inspiring teacher. It is highly unlikely, however, that such perennially curious and studious teachers are necessarily or formally researchers; if so, there would be few wonderful teachers at second level for example. Surely, indeed, it is only insofar as teachers, whether they are, contractually speaking, researchers or not, remain open and curious and able to share that passion for perennial discovery, that they will be spared burnout. Moreover, most university teachers will confirm that teaching is often not about teaching expert 'content' at all, much less about teaching one's own 'cutting edge' discoveries. What the academic needs or tries to impart or to share is often, rather, a searching need to keep learning, a need to understand so strong that it has become a way of life. Most researchers are guaranteed to be perennial learners, but beyond affirming the two equally fundamental pillars of Higher Education as being (re)searching and teaching it does not seem wise to be in any way dogmatic about the exact ways in which the two should be linked across Higher Education.

In many ways, soul-searching about how best to integrate (re)searching and teaching has been overtaken by two separate difficulties, the one currently affecting the sciences more specifically, the other the humanities. In the case of the sciences, the question concerns the channeling of academic work into industrial and commercial directions, directions explained to a degree certainly by the sheer cost of conducting research in certain scientific disciplines. Meanwhile, in the (increasingly devalued) humanities, the prospects for graduate students are so dismal in many contexts, especially perhaps the US, that many academics are unwilling to advise their students to pursue their studies further. Two American humanities scholars, Robert Koukal (Professor of Philosophy at the University of Detroit) and Thomas Benton, alias William Pannapacker, a Professor of English at Hope College) are on the record as feeling obliged to discourage the 'promising majors' who approach them about going to graduate school. In his review of Frank Donoghue's *The Last Professors*, Koukal writes that he tells such students:

> I count myself as fortunate to be a teacher of young minds, that I find my research gratifying, that I savor the intellectual stimulation of my colleagues, and that, on balance, I wouldn't trade jobs with anyone.

Why then does he discourage his students from 'making the serious commitment to pursue an advanced degree in any humanistic discipline'?

> [S]ecuring a tenure-track position is unlikely, because today well over half of those teaching college-level classes in the United States are part-time instructors, with no prospect of tenure. These positions provide an abundance of teaching, but come with low wages, no benefits, no job security, and, more often than not, no office space in which to meet students. Furthermore, adjuncts are typically deprived of any meaningful relationship with colleagues, they are provided no funding for conferences, and they are robbed of the time needed for research or any other kind of professional development.

This ground is very well-covered in Marc Bousquet's *How the University Works: Higher Education and the Low-Wage Nation* (2008) and in Thomas Benton's work (discussed further on), both of which provide cautionary reading on the casualisation of academic labour.

Apart from enabling the best possible balance between the often congruent but sometimes diverging demands of research and teaching, Higher Education is confronted by two other challenges regarding its role in research. Firstly, the issue of academic independence in the setting of research goals. And then the related issue of funding truly 'independent' academic research (especially in costlier areas). The fact is that less endowed universities will only support those research initiatives that are in line with their strategic or 'business' plans. They may tolerate other initiatives of course, but these will not be favoured. Curiously, the handful of universities, such as Oxbridge or the Ivy League colleges, that have been – and continue to be – regarded as the very best, do not, in general, publish or impose 'strategic' research plans. There may indeed be a relation of cause to effect or at least of mutual reinforcement between the academic independence of researchers at those universities and the world recognition from which those universities benefit. Such freedom is not being entertained in the international basket of crabs, however. Indeed, countries like Denmark and Finland, which have respectively one more and one fewer university than Ireland in the top-ranked 200, decided in the early to late noughties to 'raise their game' by drafting legislation limiting academic control over the setting of academic goals. Thus, according to a recent *Times Higher Education* article:

> [T]he Danish University Act of 2003, which was designed to strengthen the university sector's global competitiveness, gives departmental heads the formal power to tell individual academic staff which academic tasks to perform, and the research interests of academics must conform to the university's strategic framework. Similarly, Finland's 2009 University Act, which advocated radical changes to governance by encouraging private sector participation in university governance and altered the ten-

ure status of staff, was designed to improve universities' chances of international success.

Some Irish universities have long been engaging in similarly coercive and competitive strategising, no doubt under political pressure. However, it remains to be seen whether the outcome of such 'command and control' steroid treatment will have the desired effect in the long run or whether it will, rather, poison the academic body.

SQUARING THE FUNDING CIRCLE: MORAL ENTANGLEMENTS

Given that, even in the most comfortable and/or expensive US and UK universities, the current order is one of funding contraction, pressure and uncertainty, the plight of less cushioned institutions can only be imagined. If Higher Education is desperately chasing resources, this is not just because of the economic crisis. It is also because that crisis coincides with unprecedented political demands for competitive research outputs and for the undiscriminating growth of academic access.

It would be difficult to overestimate the extent of the desperation and its effect on standards. While the first section of this book was being drafted, the director of the London School of Economics resigned under a cloud of questions surrounding his approval of a donation of £1.5 million from Saif al Islam Gadaffy, son of the Libyan dictator Colonel Gaddafy, and also surrounding the suspicious circumstances in which an LSE doctorate had been awarded to the patron himself. Then, as already mentioned, the University of Birmingham, one of the elite Russell group of UK universities, had landed itself in hot water by pressuring academics not to be too 'academically' choosy in their recruitment of post-graduate students from overseas. This scandal is a mild echo of a serious French case of credential trafficking in which Chinese students were found to have been recruited for, and awarded, primary and Masters degrees in Business Administration in fraudulent circumstances. The latter came to light when it was discovered that the students in question couldn't speak French. This case forced the resignation in November 2009 of Laroussi Oueslati as President of the University of Toulon. An academic commission struck the former President off the French public service register in May 2010; following a criminal investigation, he was charged in September 2010 with 'passive corruption' and sentenced to a term in prison.

Meanwhile, as we saw in the previous section, in the US, some Yale University academics are horrified by the opening of a joint campus in Singapore. They are worried that this top Ivy League university's reputation for robust defence of various freedoms including academic freedom will suffer from association with the National University of Singapore (partner to Ireland's UCD in the Universitas 21 club). Certainly, the 2010 World Report of Human Rights is damning on the Singaporean government's human rights record, and specifically on its failure to meet basic standards in several critical areas including freedom of expression, association and assembly. The report notes that, while Singapore has touted its prowess as a leading economy in Southeast Asia, it does not respect the basic human rights of its own population. 'Singapore remains the textbook example of a politically repressive state,' according to Phil Robertson, deputy Asia director of Human Rights Watch.

> Individuals who want to criticise or challenge the ruling
> party's hold on power can expect to face a life of harass-
> ment, lawsuits, and even prison.

Yale academics are right to be concerned about this arranged marriage, not least because, as some of them have perhaps discovered, the managerialist regimes operated by some of the more corporate universities in the syndicate (Universitas 21) to which its new partner, the National University of Singapore, belongs, must give their syndicate associates internationally (University of Virginia or Ireland's UCD) pause for thought. I'm thinking of the practice requiring heads of department not just to give a grade at the end of the year to their colleagues' performance in teaching, research and administration, but also to rank these performances in order of merit.

University outsiders will reasonably assume that universities, when deciding how and where to do business and with whom, have access to the best available political, sociological and economic expertise, and that their governing bodies have access to suitably reliable risk assessment and risk management intelligence. But, three points need to be made about these safety nets. First, they are not foolproof. Indeed, when national, local or even internal reputational risk so often goes unidentified or ignored, as it did in the Irish universities' booby-trap bonus story, how much less likely is it that universities will be safely piloted through the moral mazes of external connections with 'foreign' interests that are often highly disputed, volatile and/or opaque? Second, national policy decisions not just on internal but also on external political, social, economic and cultural issues are typically informed by intelligence sourced in universities, rather than the other way round. However, if universities have tied themselves up into knots with commercial interests, they won't be much use in this respect, let alone in speaking truth to power. Third, anyone who knows how corporate (university) governance operates will appreciate how easily conscientious objections of principle can be neutralised.

COMMERCIALISED RESEARCH

It is easy to see how certain political pressures pose threats to intellectual freedom, making certain academic perspectives 'non grata'. For example, in *Dangerous Professors: Academic Freedom and the National Security Campus*, the authors quote a 1953 statement from a group of US university presidents to the effect that membership of the Communist Party 'extinguishes the right to a university position'. What may not be clear, however, is the way in which the commercialisation of academia can impinge just as lethally, if more indirectly, on the critical independence and intellectual legitimacy of Higher Education.

A recent statement from the incoming president of what is possibly Ireland's most independent or least bullied university succinctly warns against replacing educational by commercial priorities:

> Universities are educational organisations dedicated to the pursuit of knowledge – so while they must be pro-commercial, they will lose their way if they put commercial activities ahead of the education of students by academics who are active in research at the frontier of their disciplines (reported in *The Irish Times*, 26 August 2011).

It is important to distinguish between specific commercial and research connections linking universities with 'for profit' corporations, national or multinational, on the one hand and, on the other hand, the transformation of Higher Education *per se* into an essentially corporate system, pursuing fundamentally commercial goals (either as means or ends). It is argued right throughout this book that the simplistic managerialist structures and controls put in place in order to embed the corporate order within Higher Education are incompatible with the intrinsic educational value of enlightenment as protective of human complexities. Similarly, the commercialisation of the university results in it being turned into a corporate entity which focuses on research as a means of generating income for the institution, and on students as clients from whom resources are to be leveraged. This focus would seem to involve a fundamental corruption and *reductio ad absurdum* not just of academic standards but also of the educational mission. The process is well documented in the sources quoted throughout this book and also in the influential study by educationalists Sheila Slaughter and Gary Rhoades, entitled *Academic Capitalism and the New Economy: Markets, State, and Higher Education* (2004).

Concerning the more specific question of the commercial arrangements commonly connecting academic research, usually in the so-called 'hard' sciences, with for-profit commercial interests, as a humanities scholar I can only refer to second-hand sources. In *University, Inc.: The Corporate Corruption of Higher Education* (2005), Jennifer Washburn studies what she calls the 'threatened' realm of academic scientific research in universities.

> [T]he emergence of a utilitarian, market-model university, combined with a loud drumbeat calling on [universities and colleges] to spur national and regional economic growth, now threatens to obliterate the distinctiveness of [an] academic research culture.

Washburn goes on to observe that, within one generation, a profound shift has occurred in the reward structures for academics, and this has affected their perceptions of the intrinsic value and relative importance of various types of specifically academic research. Washburn quotes Irwin Feller, an educational economist from Pennsylvania State University, who states that over time the emphasis on patenting and generating royalties has altered the 'signals as to what constitutes productive allocation of faculty time, encouraging professors to pursue research that has patentable commercial ends'.

Washburn is of course right to point out that academic scientific research has always been associated less with its market reward than with 'priority of discovery'. She also makes the valid point that this culture of academic research had the value of 'hastening public disclosure', because the whole point was the publication of findings and the (sole) reward for the exercise was the authority and recognition derived from such publication. The distinction here is, then, between research governed by academic imperatives and research governed by proprietary imperatives that have a primarily business or industrial (and profit-based) component. However blurred that distinction becomes in some contexts – and Irish Higher Education's present or past joint pharmaceutical development programmes with companies such as Elan or Servier seem to illustrate that fuzziness – it is surely only logical to imagine that the academic end of the research culture spectrum might allow for more flexibility and freedom and thus for more opportunistic breakthroughs. One distinguished neuroscientist, Donald Stein from Emory University, is quoted on this subject by Jennifer Washburn. Stein is Professor of Emergency Medicine at Emory and has been credited with pioneering the use of the reproductive hormone progesterone for the treatment of brain trauma. He contrasts the current situation with the one that pertained in Higher Education when he was first employed as an academic.

> [Back then] most people believed that they were doing what they were doing – generating ideas and discoveries – because of the public good.

If Stein considers that academic medical research today is unduly influenced by external corporate (that is, commercial) interests, there is certainly some evidence to suggest that he may be right. One could cite the recent Duke University cancer research scandal commented upon in detail in *The Economist* of 8 September 2011.

> The university's lapses and errors included being slow to deal with potential financial conflicts of interest declared by [its academic researchers], including involvement in Expression Analysis Inc and CancerGuide DX, two firms to which the university also had ties.

The Duke case was particularly invidious, leading to class actions by cancer patients against the university, because clinical trials had been engaged based on the falsified Duke research findings.

The issue of 'corporate capture' is especially sensitive when it involves, as medical research often does, matters of life and death. This is why 'bioethics' is a flourishing academic field in itself. So much so that there is some controversy at present about the 'ethics' of the pharma industry sponsoring – or even directly employing – bioethics academics. Howard Brody is the author of a blog on this subject and of a book entitled *Hooked: Ethics, the Medical Profession and the Pharmaceutical Industry*. Brody explains that there are two schools of thought regarding 'corporate capture'. The first maintains that transparency regarding bioethical issues and disclosure of conflicts of interests suffice to address the risks involved; the second is that only disinvestment, or a separation of interests, will avert the worst. Brody himself is highly skeptical of the direction being taken by the research ethics 'business'.

Although, like Brody, Stein ecognises the wider implications of the 'corporate capture' of academic research, he seems to be most fearful about the perverse effect exerted on *education specifically* by this cultural change in academia.

> Now when you go and look at university business plans, as they are called, students are seen as clients; patients are seen as customers. . . . The question has now become 'What is going to sell?' as opposed to 'What is the right thing to teach? . . . Once things take on commercial, monetary value, the whole academic decision-making structure becomes impacted.

Referring to the university administrations which are themselves caught in the vice-grip of commercialisation pressures, Stein notes that 'they strategise about the university's brand name and niche market, its competitive edge and pricing strategies', only paying lip-service, according to him, to educational priorities, the real priority being commercialised research:

> All of the reward structures, higher salaries, merit increases, travel to scientific and professional meetings. . . . You have to be deprived of all your sensory apparatus not to see what is going on. . . .The real commitment is to the research scholarship – and the generation of indirect costs.

The expression 'indirect costs' refers to the fact that, when university researchers make successful bids for funding, a certain percentage, in fact a very high fraction (more than one-fifth, typically) of the funds that come in to the university in order to pay for the research in question (the people, the apparatus, and so on) gets bitten off by the university's research office as recovery of the indirect or infrastructural costs incurred by the institution. On large contracts, this amounts to significant income for the university and that's not counting its patenting or licensing income, permitted in the US for example under the famous Bayh-Dole Act of 1980, which allowed universities to pursue ownership of research innovations.

It would surely be an exaggeration to claim that the freedom of universities from market constraints allowed them in the past to be absolute havens for the type of open-ended or blue-sky fundamental research that led to countless significant, serendipitous scientific discoveries. Yet Jennifer Washburn is no doubt right about the state of academic science today.

> [T]he line between academic and commercial science [is dissolved today], as the openness of academic culture gives way to a proprietary one [and] as professors are encouraged to think more and more like entrepreneurs.

Although she suggests that the university is 'too important a public institution to be surrendered to the narrow dictates of the market', Washburn does not overstate her case. She does not deny, for example, that US universities are what they are today largely because so many of them were built up in tandem with the interests of the US military/industrial complex. Nor does she claim that industrially sponsored research is worse than no research at all. Simply, in her view, and clearly in the view also of at least one current Irish university president, commercial imperatives need to be kept in check in the Higher Education context.

The history of pharma scandals shows just how catastrophic the consequences can be when commercial interests trump all other fundamental values. The more buoyant industrial and commercial spheres are usually well able to absorb the portfolio setbacks and financial penalties involved when harmful conflicts of interests or values are not picked up in time. But are Higher Education institutions equally immune? Because part of the core mission of universities is research, and because some kinds of scientific research are so expensive and so multilateral, the case for direct industrial sponsorship may appear to be open and shut. Although this seems to be the predominant view across the corporate university world, some informed discussions of the issue suggest otherwise. Thus, in his much-quoted study, *Ivory Tower and Industrial Innovation: University-Industry Technology* (2004), David Mowery is broadly favourable to universities supporting patenting and licensing, but only if universities recognise that 'technology transfer' is subsidiary to 'their central institutional missions of education and research'. Mowery does further note the disproportionate share of university licensing and patenting accounted for by the biomedical area. And he is concerned that, when it comes to practice, Higher Education decision-making tends to be entrusted to those for whom the most valuable research is that which promises or realises the greatest commercial potential. The pertinence of that concern is well illustrated by the predominant bio-medical or bio-technological orientation and expertise of the Washington/Huron Advisory

Group, and indeed the bio-medical background of the current presidents of at least four major Irish universities/colleges. Mowery's concerns are particularly obvious in his enjoinders to US university administrations.

> [University administrators should] heed the concerns raised by their predecessors during the 1930s and 1940s over the political risks created by any appearance of university 'profiteering' from patenting and licensing.

Furthermore, he suggests that:

> US universities, no less than universities in other nations, will retain their privileged institutional status as entities that deserve extensive public financial support and prestige to the extent that they are seen by the public as serving its broad interests. The single-minded pursuit of revenue is not always consistent with this lofty position . . . and universities must take care to ensure that their core missions are not put at risk.

Mowery was writing this, of course, before the collapse of US public finances. In that context, the risk to 'core missions' can only escalate.

So what are the implications of Higher Education institutions accepting sponsorship from companies which turn out to be implicated in breaches of ethical or even legal codes? And how should a university respond if it finds itself in such a situation? Isn't this what appears to have happened in the case of the highly successful Irish-owned pharmaceutical company, Elan, once a key industrial partner of one of Ireland's major universities? In fact, Elan's HQ was located on the campus of the university and the chair of the university's governing authority was on the board of Elan (and of United Drug as well). Elan's stock plummeted when the company's reputation was affected by an accounting scandal and even worse by an ethical disaster with a drug called Zonegran, a disaster credited by an *Irish Independent* editorial as late as 17 December 2010 as having caused 'the strong smell that . . . emanated from Elan for years'. With Elan currently showing signs of recovering its buoyancy, the company is once again publicly involved with Irish university research, donating for example 3 million euro to sponsor Europe's 'first interdisciplinary chair in the Business of Biotechnology'. Although private industrial sponsorship of academic posts is rife in the US, and is common also in the UK corporate university system, such links between private industry and academic research are not universal practice in Higher Education. In France, for example, there is little or no direct industrial sponsorship of academic research or education. Up to now, for example, it is difficult to imagine a French university founding, as the University of Oxford did to a major outcry in 2011, a professorship of marketing sponsored by the huge cosmetic company L'Oréal. It would also be unthinkable, at least up to now, for a French university to open a 'School of Drug Development'. Indeed, the academic-industrial traffic seems to flow in the other direction in France, so that top scientists working for the major French – or principally French – pharma companies like Sanofi (ex-Aventis, itself formed from a merger of Rhône-Poulenc with a German company), often act as pro bono external examiners for academic research projects.

This difference is all the more interesting in view of the fact that another French-owned drug pharma company (Servier) has been a major pharmaceutical sponsor of at least one Irish university's academic research in the area of translational medicine (medicine that shortens the path leading from laboratory research to the patient, via drug development, clinical trials and so on). In 2007 the company invested €7.5 million in the university's drug development research. Unfortunately, Servier is currently beset by difficulties which dwarf by some distance those that almost undid Elan. The company was suspended by the French Drug Industry Association (LEEM) in January 2011 and a trial has been set for the end of 2012. The company will face four criminal charges: preventable pharmaceutical manslaughter of between 500 and 2,000 people in France; deception regarding the alleged mis-description of a drug called Médiator; and defrauding medical insurers, principally the French state, of up to €1 billion. The fourth charge is one of corruption, since it is alleged that Servier used political connections holding business interests in the company to influence regulatory bodies in its favour. Some indication of the way in which the French academic world views the situation (in which Servier is, of course, innocent until proven guilty) was given by an announcement made by the University of Aix-Marseille II in April 2011 after the release of the report issuing from a preliminary state investigation into the affair. The university, which had given its graduating Pharmacy Class of 2010 the name 'Jacques Servier', took the unusual step of withdrawing the name and rebaptising the class of 2010. Clearly, though, such a cut and dried response is quite impossible in the situation pertaining in some Irish universities, where academic research is routinely sponsored by deeply embedded, private, for-profit interests, and as such has no doubt come to rely upon a whole tissue of interconnections and interdependency between academic and industrial science.

Although the stakes of this subject lie immeasurably far beyond this author's understanding or competence, it is nonetheless interesting that shortly before *Academic Armageddon* went to press, the latest book of an Irish-educated Professor of Psychiatry at the University of Cardiff, David Healy, appeared in print. Its title? *Pharmageddon*.

TOTAL 'CORPORATE CAPTURE'

For many commentators, managerialism rather than commercialism is the hallmark of academic endgame. In *Knowledge, Higher Education, and the New Managerialism* (edited by Rosemary Deem, Sam Hillyard and Mike Reed), managerialism is defined as a dogma according to which management is 'necessarily better than any other [way of] rationally coordinating and controlling collective action in a modern society'. From the managerialist perspective, management is considered to be 'necessarily, technically and socially superior to any other conceivable form of social practice and organisation such as craft, profession, or community'. It just never seems to occur to anybody that there might be far more humane, far more creative, constructive and productive ways of organising work and life. The managerialist mindset is driven above all by what Deem et al. call 'market populism' or 'consumer democracy'. Currently all-pervasive, managerialism is at the heart of most public service reform in the West. The problem is, however, that line management has a vaguely militaristic, hierarchical cachet that is arguably anachronistic, given that many contemporary business corporations have moved away from vertical structuring. In Higher Education, managerialism has restructured academic life into a system of strategic and operational control. In a coup that looks something like the French revolution in reverse, managerialism subjected the academic body politic to a proliferation of 'heads'. It has never been clear, of course, how this proliferation is meant to a) save money or b) improve the 'performance' of some of the most finely-tuned minds society has to offer. Some of these, the minds of cultural critics, linguists, botanists, sociologists, biochemists, physicists, mathematicians, classicists, musicologists, political scientists, etc. have been manoeuvred into positions where everything that they should stand for risks being sucked into a vortex. The shallowness of the resulting culture is captured by the title of Gaye Tuchmann's book on the subject: *Wannabe U: Inside the Corporate University* (2009).

By far the most noticeable aspect of managerialism, especially rampant in the UK university system and its 'derivatives' in Australia and Ireland, for example, is the extremely time-consuming routine of 'accountability' procedures: performance and quality reviews, for example, and audits or 'full economic costing exercises'. Some academics may view these operations as necessary evils; others may despise them as inane busy-work. Arguably, though, they are dangerous. Not so much because they seek to measure things that are immeasurable. Rather because they seek to measure things that are actually destroyed by attempted measurement. How on earth could we measure how (usefully) critical, how genuinely independent, how creatively contrarian, how uniquely insubordinate, how much of a maverick or a genius a given academic or academic unit has been in a given year? This is, of course, a purely rhetorical question. The fact is that managerialist regimes are allergic to critical independence. Which begs the disturbing question as to what exactly is being managed and measured in the micro-management of academic work. Apart, that is, from the invertebrate virtues of conformity and compliance. In an article that will be discussed further on, two Australian academics argue that university managerialism produces amenability and virtually guarantees that critique and creative innovation are foreclosed rather than encouraged. They contend that 'risk management then becomes, for the individual, the management of the risk to oneself of non-compliance, of non-viability within the audited policies and practices of the institution'.

In his book *The Fall of the Faculty: The All-Adminstrative University*, already mentioned in the previous section, Benjamin Ginsberg outlines the managerialist ethos that has invaded the US public university system.

> Universities are filled with armies of functionaries: the vice presidents, associate vice presidents, assistant vice presidents, provosts, associate provosts, vice provosts, assistant provosts, deans, deanlets, deanlings, each commanding staffers and assistants, who, more and more, direct [operations]. Backed by their administrative legions, university presidents and other senior administrators have been able, at most schools, to dispense with faculty

involvement in campus management, and thereby to reduce the faculty's influence in university affairs. At some schools, the faculty has already surrendered and is hoping that the Geneva convention will protect it from waterboarding. . . . There is hardly a university today that is not suffering from rampant administrative blight. In battles with the faculty, administrators sometimes win because they are clever; more often they win because there are so many of them and, having little to do, they are free to focus on bureaucratic struggle while the faculty is occupied in its classrooms, libraries and laboratories and refuses to commit its time to the effort.

The 'waterboarding' remark has to be read as evidence of the degree of maddened infuriation inspired in academics like Ginsberg by the phenomenon that he is analysing. He is most concerned, however, to communicate the importance for the general public of what he is so angry about.

The general public has a stake in the quality of America's colleges and universities, and the question of who controls the university has a direct and immediate impact on institutional quality. Former Harvard dean Henry Rosovsky once observed that the quality of a [university] is likely to be 'negatively correlated with the unrestrained power of administrators'.

Ginsberg argues that when 'controlled by administrators' the university is denatured.

[The all-administrative university can] never be more than what Stanley Aronowitz has aptly termed a knowledge factory, offering more or less sophisticated forms of vocational training to meet the needs of other established institutions in the public and private sectors.

Wesley Shumar's *College for Sale: A Critique of the Commodification of Higher Education* makes a very similar point.

> A sterile administrative culture concerned only with managing problems and controlling people, not only exacts control but produces alienation in its wake.

Shumar outlines the situation where university administrations, faced with a funding shortfall and a debt crisis, regard micro-management as the only answer. The result is inevitable.

> [P]art-timers are exploited, students feel alienated and just there to get the credential; learning, knowledge and political participation are not much on anyone's mind.

He goes on to predict how universities may develop. 'Perhaps the image to come is one of faculty as pieceworkers in an international system of knowledge and technologies,' before concluding that all academics, social scientists in particular, really should urgently examine how our universities are working at present.

> Reflexive political practice is necessary in order to effectively raise a voice against the dominant movement in American capitalism. Currently, we favour the survival of systems, corporations and bureaucratic institutions over the well-being and lives of people. If we are to survive the coming century we will need to humanise these forces and prioritise people over things. Universities need to reinvigorate the quest for knowledge: knowledge that serves the interests of people, brings healing and benefit to the planet and re-establishes a concern for human values. This will only happen if university intellectuals become aware of the institutions in which they work and the global pressures on those institutions.

Such awareness initiatives do exist. For example, the CORES group (Committee for Open Research on Economy and Society) was formed by a group of concerned academics opposed to the naming of a University of Chicago research institute after Milton Friedman. However, the committee gradually expanded into a much bigger project of resistance to the modus operandi of the corporate university. It is worth quoting the following long extract from the petition that the group sent to the President of their university. The entire controversy, which played out in 2008, is reported in the electronic publication *The Chicago Maroon*. If the length of the quote seems excessive, readers should know that it is probably the most accurate description they will ever find of the administrative model of corporate universities world-wide. The following are, for the CORES, the key corporate features of their university's administration.

- Centralised management, where decisions affecting the academic quality of the University are handed down as faits accomplis;

- . . . Statutory organs of faculty governance . . . have become theatres for staging an uninformed and meaningless consent;

- Withholding of crucial information, particularly anything that – if known – could threaten the administration's projects (with strategically-timed dumps of such information over the summer or at end of term, when the faculty cannot respond);

- Initiatives whose prime appeal is their fund-raising potential, developed by an ever-growing cadre of administrators without significant academic experience or deep understanding of academic values;

- A business mentality, in which academic units are understood – even designed – to function as product lines and profit centers;

- A systematic reversal of ends and means, so that academic activity becomes a means to raise money, rather than money being the means to advance knowledge;

- A habitual willingness to turn a blind eye when financial interests threaten to compromise, deform, and eclipse intellectual and moral concerns.

What we see is the accelerating transformation of the University into a profit-seeking enterprise steered by savvy managers, locked in competition with its business rivals (aka peer institutions) for large investors (aka donors and grants), brands, markets, products, and outlets (aka new campuses, institutes, degree programs, online systems), skilled workers (aka faculty), and consumers (aka students). Such corporatisation of the academy involves dramatic restructuring of the way the academy is organised and functions. Crucial decisions are ever more frequently made by administration, not faculty, and made on the basis of what will bring in the money.

The ultimate effect of this is to shift power to the donors whose favor [is courted by] the administrators: a recipe for the corruption of intellectual life. The university becomes an instrument through which other kinds of actors – some well-intentioned, and some decidedly not – seek to advance their own pet projects and interests.

[Certain] processes – administrative centralisation, entrepreneurial pursuit of profit, evasion and effacement of faculty control – now threaten the University as a whole, as is seen at numerous flashpoints. . . . Few, if any, have been presented to the Faculty Council or other governing bodies for deliberation or a vote.

- Metastatic growth of administrative staff (especially at the Vice Presidential level);

- Withholding of budget and other information from the faculty's governing bodies;

- Expansion of revenue-generating terminal MA programs at the expense of PhD programs;

- Increasingly centralised control over levels of graduate admissions . . .

- Administrative interference with academic matters (curriculum, appointments) . . .

- Without consent of the faculty Senate, who are statutorily charged with exclusive jurisdiction in such matters, University administration accepted the establishment of a Confucius Institute, an academically and politically ambiguous initiative sponsored by the government of the People's Republic of China. Proceeding without due care to ensure the Institute's academic integrity, it has risked having the University's reputation legitimate the spread of such Confucius Institutes in this country and beyond.

The University of Chicago is particularly invested, as already indicated, in graduate education. As we will see further on in this section, many US academics are far less exercised about the governance issues raised by CORES than about the corporate university's effects on the standards of undergraduate education specifically. It should be quite clear, however, that the two sets of problems (academic governance and academic standards) are in fact intimately linked. What unites them is the fundamental incompatibility between a) an idealistic view of education as enlightenment (rather than as a business to be managed) and b) the subjection of academic effort, both research and education, to a failed ideology of markets as the self-servicing engines of all human endeavour and interaction.

In their book *The Enterprise University: Power, Governance and Reinvention in Australia* (Cambridge 2000), Mark Considine and Simon Marginson tell essentially the same story of the rise of a business culture and executive-style organisation within antepodean universities. However, another pair of Australian academics, this time from the University of Western Sydney, have produced a particularly convincing indictment of the mechanisms and effects of managerialism in Australian universities which, as already indicated, followed from the start the UK rather than the US model. Bronwyn Davies and Peter Bansel's article, entitled 'Governmentality and Academic Work: Shaping the Hearts and Minds of Academic Workers' appeared in the *Journal of Curriculum Theorizing* in 2010. It opens with the following statement:

> The single most important feature of neo-liberal government is that it systematically dismantles the will to critique, thus potentially shifting the very nature of what a university is and the ways in which academics understand their work.

In the following extract, the authors quote Derek Bok (the ex-President of Harvard mentioned in Section 1) in support of their thesis.

> Within neo-liberal mentalities of government, 'welfare' or 'government responsibility for the well-being of the people' becomes a 'degraded mentality', whereas 'competitive market mentalities are elevated'. Indeed 'the market becomes the singular discourse through which individual and institutional acceptability will be recognised'.

The general aim of Davies' and Bansel's article is to explain how neo-liberalism operates.

> [We aim to] make some headway in dismantling the sense of inevitability that neo-liberal practices of government appear to have generated both within the university sector and in other work sites.

The two researchers argue that managerialism serves a fundamentally neo-liberal, free-market goal and it does so in three simple ways. First by measuring academic value:

> All products are redefined in terms of their dollar [or] exchange value. Rather than valuing the product in its own terms (a book that opens up new ways of thinking, for example), financial or pseudo-financial calculations are made for the purpose of facilitating economic flows.

The authors explain in detail the metrics of the Australian research assessment exercise, which mirrors faithfully the one used in the UK. Although no national RAE (research assessment exercise) is applied in Ireland since there is, nationally, insufficient critical mass to make it meaningful, a broadly similar 'credit' system or 'resource allocation model' is widely applied in Irish Higher Education for the purposes of working out the share of the funding cake that should be given to individual academic units, and for figuring out the promotional worth of individual academic units or individuals.

> In Australian universities . . . a book's worth is uniformly calculated as 6 points (less if it's an edited book) and points are made meaningful through being given dollar values, which in turn translate into government funding to the university, and into points scored for the calculation of teaching loads and research status.

The second axis of managerialism is competitiveness:

> Through setting individuals against each other in intensified competitive systems of funding with clearly identified measures of success, . . . individuals are de-individualised and converted into generic members of an auditable group.

And the third hallmark of neo-liberalism is its determination to collapse 'the critical gap between the liberal subject and government'.

> Whereas the liberal subject had as part of its responsibility the maintenance of a distance from government and a responsibility to call it to account, the neo-liberal subject does not.

Davies and Bandel argue that whereas liberalism (as in the 'liberal arts and sciences') can function as a critique of state reason or as a kind of 'doctrine of limitation' of state power, neo-liberalism abolishes the gap in which critique can function. They quote perhaps the most important late twentieth-century French philosopher, Michel Foucault, who devoted his life to a study of the relation between power and knowledge. For Foucault, it is through critical thought that human beings try to establish what is true and what is false and that they become 'knowing beings'. And it is as 'knowing beings' that humans accept or reject rules as ethical or not. For Davies and Bansel, however, the reformed university's modus operandi is governed not by focusing on knowledge or critical thinking, but by deploying 'audit technologies'.

> [These technologies] classify and diagnose populations of workers and the potential risks in managing them. Discourses of efficiency and quality, for example, regularise academic practice, narrowly defining values and successes in order to render them measurable. Academics are persuaded to teach the same way, complete the same forms, make applications to the same funding bodies, make links with industry – in short to reproduce the same practices in order to reorganise themselves to fit the template of best practice as this is defined by management.

If this really is the model of academia which corresponds to the wishes of 'populist' or 'consumer' democracy identified by Rosemary Deem and her co-authors as being in the ascendant in today's world, then the only important question that remains to be answered is whether or not 'the people' insisting on what passes nowadays for 'educational reform' know what they're wishing for.

Nobody who cares about the standards of Higher Education could be sanguine about the idea that the latter are being compromised by inappropriate accountancy practices.

> [These] practices of accountancy cannot recognise or countenance anyone who sees their job as responsibly working against the grain of dominant discourses, of asking dangerous questions of government, of opening up the spaces of difference where new possibilities might emerge from the previously unthought or unknown.

Is it true, though, that corporate universities near and far have transformed academics, as Davies and Bansel claim, into 'anxious' and 'self-censoring' individuals? Well, is it true that such universities constantly bombard academic staff with e-communications designed to elicit compliance? Is it true that they issue their academic staff with endless invitations, enjoinders or even instructions to 'improve' or 'enhance' their teaching performance? Is it true that they pressure them to produce and to publish research results regardless of how under-baked these may be? Is it true that they pressure them to respond to 'client satisfaction' feedback by modifying course content? Is it true that they increasingly require academics to venture outside their field of competence into more consumer-friendly border-crossing areas? Is it true that they insist on adapting assessment procedures to client expectations and convenience? That they require grading to be kept in line with student retention targets?

A classic effect of that bombardment is a sort of going-with-the-flow or switching off. And again, the loss is not that of academics themselves. To put it more baldly, when academics work in a context where administrators are awarded remunerative incentives to recruit income-generating students, and where governments reward plumped-up student retention and graduation rates, it will become even more difficult than it already is to ensure that the only students recruited are those who show that they have the potential to benefit from rigorous academic study and to attain certain standards. And it will remain impossible to ensure that students will only progress and graduate if they can show that they have attained those standards.

THE HUMANITIES IMPERILLED

In a culture where commercial concerns trump all others, the old adage holds particularly true: the 'chosen' and cherished disciplines will be those that make money, attract (sponsorship) money or study money. If ailing subjects or squeezed disciplines falling outside the commercial pale would not even be prayed for in some Irish universities, this is not necessarily because the latter are particularly philistine institutions. Rather, all corporate universities seem to work in this way. Usually, indeed, in the carefully cloned corporate university every last detail of university governance, structures, processes and self-promotion is predicated on the commercial model and so, despite the varying thicknesses of the veneer of civility and despite varying degrees of lip-service to the cross-subsidising of academic interests, disciplines with significantly lesser (or no) commercialisation value are bound to be sidelined, bullied and/or starved.

Even if some humanities disciplines have managed to stay afloat in most universities, Jennifer Washburn refers to a 'national trend' of imperilled disciplines in the US.

> Across the country, schools looking to trim their budgets
> are targeting programs in history, foreign languages, and

journalism or are combining disciplines like philosophy, religion, and political science into one pared-down department.

Even if this is by no means the first time that the map of humanities disciplines has been redrawn, Washburn is right to observe that, unlike previous shifts, today's challenges to the humanities 'are being driven not by intellectual concerns but by financial considerations and pure market demand'.

> When the criteria for judging an academic discipline centre on how much money [academics] can generate through grants and corporate sponsorship, most humanities departments invariably find it difficult to compete.

What happens when wealth creation and/or training for the job market becomes the exclusive focus of universities? Traditionally, the primacy of such a narrowly utilitarian focus is challenged especially, but not exclusively, from within the humanities disciplines. Sometimes, however, ex-free marketeers do penance for past blindness by emphasising the value and importance of the humanities. Jennifer Washburn approvingly quotes Alan Greenspan, former chairman of the US Federal Reserve, in this connection. Referring to the so-called 'knowledge-based' economy, Greenspan notes that in the future 'the ability to think abstractly will be increasingly important across a broad range of professions'.

> A remarkable and broad presumption [persists] that the ability to think conceptually is fostered through exposure to philosophy, literature, music, art and languages. Most great conceptual advances are interdisciplinary and involve synergies of different specialities.

This is, of course, a fundamentally utilitarian argument to the effect that a bit of culture can enhance general human productivity. Greenspan does, however, add a note of complete anti-utilitarianism to his words of praise for education in the liberal arts, recognising that the latter 'embody more than a means of increasing technical intellectual efficiency'.

> They encourage the appreciation of life experiences that reach beyond material well-being and indeed are comparable and mutually reinforcing. Its goal is not to serve as a subcontractor for the market.

To the unsuspecting, Greenspan's patter may appear to strike a magnanimous blow for the humanities. This was, after all, exactly the kind of velvet talk that accompanied the killer blow dealt to the humanities during the toxic corporate reforms that undid certain Irish universities. Apparently replying to those who at least have the honesty to make the impossible demand that the humanities earn their keep, Greenspan defends their place in educating 'a broad range of professions' to think innovatively and thereby to 'work smarter'. He also recognises that the arts and humanities enhance non-material well-being by enabling an appreciation of the finer things of life.

In other words, Greenspan's version of the arts and humanities reduces them to light refreshment for economic warriors. It divorces the humanities from their true value, namely, critical and independent thinking in the service of thought itself and of truth and justice. But then this is arguably the very link that has been broken by the view of the world so ably promoted by Greenspan himself before, during and after the economic crash. So, although he may appear to be doing penance for the gung-ho sins of neo-liberalism by reciting a few 'Hail Humanities', it is still quite clear that he takes a winner's and even a consumer's view of both the material and the non-material well-being enabled by the humanities.

The cost of that 'winner takes all' distortion is ably described by Martha Nussbaum in her recent book, *Not for Profit: Why Democracy Needs the Humanities* (2010). Nussbaum, professor of

Law and Ethics at the University of Chicago, argues that the humanities have traditionally been seen as a central resource for the generation and support of a democratic model of citizenship. According to her, however, this vision was blasted out of US universities as the latter began to see the sole purpose of the humanities as boosting national economic growth. For Nussbaum, as for others, the primary difficulty with this economic imperative is that the education deemed to facilitate economic productivity does not necessarily, or does not typically, have as a priority the inculcation of a democratic, let alone a critical or empathetic civic or humane perspective. One important dimension of Nussbaum's book is its study of certain educational models currently being tested on the Indian sub-continent as an alternative to the all-too-familiar corporate model predominant globally.

In one way, Nussbaum takes no less instrumentalist a view of the humanities than Greenspan or other proponents of the 'knowledge economy', when they sing the praises of the humanities as a training in the thinking essential for innovation. However, for Nussbaum, the humanities serve an ethical and political ideal of justice for all rather than material benefit or cultural patina for the many. For her, the primary benefits of the humanities derive from their focus not just on what is cognitively wrong and right, true or false, possible or impossible, certain or uncertain, but also on what is right in the sense of just, ethical or humane. In other words, she believes that the humanities address the issue of our deepest ideals. Nussbaum's view is related to that of the American historian Richard Hofstadter who – already in the 1950s – saw Higher Education as being called upon to look beyond servicing, and certainly beyond servicing an economy. Hofstadter goes even further:

> The best reason for supporting the college and the university lies not in the services they can perform, vital though such services may be, but in the values they represent. The ultimate criterion of the place of higher learning in Ameri-

ca will be the extent to which it is esteemed not as a necessary instrument of external ends, but as an end in itself.

Similarly, in his recent book *College: What It Was, Is and Should Be* (2012), Andrew Delbanco, chair of American Studies at Columbia University, concludes that a college education can only be properly meaningful when it is not instrumentalised, that is, treated as the means to an unrelated end (prosperity, prestige, and so on).

The pressures drowning out voices like Delbanco's and Nussbaum's are part of the global curtailment or even destruction of the political domain per se and of its absorption into a purely economic maelstrom. One of the clearest signs of this contraction of the political sphere is the lack of influence of national politics and politicians in the face of the deeply anti-democratic transnational forces moving not just financial capital but also arms and drugs around the world. Another sign is the way in which whole states have been turned into serf economies, essentially serving opaque but transcendent financial interests. The issue is not just that academia is being forced to conform (as it always did) to certain economic targets and goals. It is rather that these goals and targets are not being set openly. They are not being debated and decided internally or democratically, by university presidents, senates or faculties, nor even by local, regional or national quangos or governments, but are rather being ordained 'globally', by the apparently uncoordinated, unnamed market forces that are moving everything, including educational traffic, everywhere.

CORPORATE CAPITULATION

One of the most cogent studies to date of the effect on the humanities specifically of this rise of corporate culture is *The Last Professors: The Corporate University and the Fate of the Humanities* (2008) by a Ohio State University academic, Frank Donoghue. The focus of the book is on US humanities professors.

These are tenured scholars who, usually following about eight years in a 'tenure track' position, are granted the job security guaranteed by full tenure. Donoghue believes that US humanities academics have been terminally compromised by the 'dynamics of the corporate university'. For him, they have already lost the power to save either themselves or the humanities and are marching towards extinction. He further argues that they have been complicit in their own demise.

Frank Donoghue charts capitalism's historical ambivalence and even hostility towards the humanities. He shows how, from the Golden Age of US university expansion right up to the present day, the rule of business discourse and methods has always served to challenge if not to undermine the role of the humanities. However, Donoghue believes that in today's world, the ideology of utilitarian efficiency and productivity has effectively taken over academia absolutely, driving the Humanities into a terminally defensive position.

The core of the problem is that, in order to survive, the humanities have had to justify the study of philosophy or history, language or literature as a 'market-smart' move. As we have seen, even the most plausible advocates of the humanities, such as Alan Greenspan, defend the arts and humanities mainly with reference to criteria of economic 'usefulness'. This has meant, in general, that the humanities have tried to 'fit in somehow' into the corporatised university environment. It is not surprising that humanities academics were reluctant to trumpet their constitutional discomfort with the supremacy of 'market-smart' thinking. It is quite understandable that they would have tried instead to join in the game, organising themselves into research groups, research teams, research clusters (or whatever the relevant buzzword was). It is completely understandable too that they would have accepted the disciplinary or inter-disciplinary reformatting of their teaching. Not merely so that they too could advertise their courses for their market exchange value, in terms that the market would recognise and buy; not merely so that they too could bid for impressive-sounding funding grants and call themselves 'principal investigators' as the research industry nomenclature has it. But also for the best of reasons: for example, that they might encourage particularly gifted humanities students to choose a future in academia. More generally, humanities scholars were aware that, in the absence of such 'join them' tactics, their disciplines would be 'put out to pasture' progressively and in some cases summarily evicted. Some universities already don't bother much with the humanities: for example the King Abdullah University of Science and Technology in Saudi Arabia. It is telling that this college, to which, according to itself, 'the Advisory Group has served as the primary academic and global research adviser', has as its President the ex-CEO of the National University of Singapore. Furthermore, according to a 2009 article in *Times Higher Education*, this university is backed by partnerships with Imperial College London, as well as Oxford and Cambridge. Not only that, but the *THE* article quotes the founders of the university as promising, in a Humpty-Dumpty-ish turn of phrase, that King Abdullah University is destined to be 'the most independent university in the world'.

The fact is, though, that very, very few universities scrap the humanities altogether. It is not, then, the outright omission of the humanities from the world's university menus that is making some humanities academics see their species as having come to the verge of extinction in the US. What is it, then, that is far more toxic to these disciplines than eviction or omission? To answer this question, the analogy of genetic modification is helpful. When humans declared primal biocidal warfare on undesirable organisms, the latters' DNA mutated and our weedkillers and antibiotics produced pests that were even stronger and more resistant. Conversely, the surest way of neutralising any lifeforce is by introducing a genetic modification that makes the organism either incompatible with life or unable to interfere with our plans. Reprogramming or reengineering is a form of denaturing and this is how corporate culture has poisoned the humanities within Higher Education. Donoghue shows how corporate values were internalised by academics in the humanities, just as they were by academics working across all disciplines. Thus, instead of continuing to live and work by the values traditionally defended or treasured by the humanities – the critical re-interpretation of ways of thinking about being human, for example – many humanities academics obediently began to allow market values like productivity, efficiency, and competitive achievement to drive their efforts too. The extent to which this extraordinary surrender polluted what had traditionally been the ideals of the humanities (civic responsibility and existential fulfillment, for example) cannot be overestimated.

As we have already seen, in the US, despite an overall expansion in university labour, the proportion of tenured academic positions shrank rather than expanding. The weak humanities job market forced humanities scholars to sell themselves feverishly not just to be appointed to tenure-track positions, but then to be awarded tenure (in the US, the tenure process is traditionally a long, gruelling haul, often fraught with disappointments as collegially corrosive as they are individually destructive). An extraordinary level of competition for the prize of fully tenured positions, along with a glut of PhDs, necessarily created the need for supposedly uniform measures of comparative academic achievement. As Donoghue points out, however, uniform metrics can tend, in turn, to produce fairly uniform scholarship. This is probably why the UK's 'Research Assessment Exercise' has been refocused as the 'Research Excellence Framework'. In its previous incarnation, this exercise was blamed for the flooding of the academic publication market with sub-par work. The re-engineering of UK research assessment towards 'impact measurement' will not solve the fundamental problem, however, as Fred Inglis's attack quoted in Section One makes perfectly clear.

When the focus of humanities academics themselves, as 'guides' to what it means to be 'human', is on winning a prize that is not 'knowledge', or 'wisdom' or 'discernment' or 'education', but a proxy prize – a title, a grade, research impact credit etc – then how can they connect their work or encourage students to connect their work with the timeless humanities project of deepening our understanding of our humanity? The answer is simple. They can't.

The Last Professors paints a grim future for the humanities. Donoghue fears that few traditional universities will be able to afford to offer an education in humanities subjects, other than as an instrumentalised veneer of modular culture, as shallow as it is commodified. As for the 'prestige' institutions which will retain humanities disciplines, the latter will be just as subordinated as technological disciplines, and possibly even more catastrophically so, to the genetic destructiveness of credentialism and the pursuit of commodified prestige. In fact, Donoghue's future has arrived as close to home as London in the shape of the already mentioned 'New College of the Humanities' planned for 2012 by Anthony Grayling et al. Widely opposed by a broad spectrum of British academics, this new venture has been called in the Higher Education media a sham, an empty 'branding exercise with purchased celebrity endorsements and a PR-driven website'. All told, if it shortly becomes operational as planned, this institution will be an incomparable UK monument to educational proxy and to the self-immolation of UK humanities on the altar of a Higher Education market gone mad.

FROM EDUCATION TO SALESMANSHIP: THE FALLOUT

Along with the casualisation of academic labour, another important feature of the corporatised university is, as we have seen, the growing gap between administration/management and front-line academics. A managerialist monopoly has apparently managed to impose itself effortlessly in the corporate university worldwide, although academics have not always been slow to point out the implications. Jennifer Washburn quotes the dismay of one East Carolina professor of English.

> Not to put too fine a point on it, the dean by fiat seemed to rewrite our professional self-definition, from scholarship to salesmanship.

This particular administrator, dean of the College of Arts and Sciences of the University of East Carolina, had amended the criteria for the yearly evaluations of tenured academics. The significance of these yearly evaluations is that they determine the granting (or not) of salary raises. The adjustment involved an increased emphasis on bringing in research funding, such that submitting four grant proposals (that is, four applications for research funding) would henceforth be regarded as the equivalent of publishing one scholarly article.

In some universities, (truly) leading administrators prefer to resign rather than act as enforcers of policies which horrify them. Again, Washburn quotes a case that arose in New School University, where the dean of the Faculty of Political and Social Science found his position untenable in a context where he believed that the administration was subordinating 'academic values to market values'. The straw that broke the camel's back was a proposal by the school's provost that private bonuses be paid to deans who boosted the tuition-fee paying cohort of admissions. The size of the bonus would correspond to the number of fee-paying students a dean could bring in. With the exception of the latter refinement (pro rata incentive scheme, amounting to a fairly primitive commission basis), this is not very different from the 'bonus bonanza' as its operation and justification were self-described in the Irish case mentioned in Section 1. Unlike the dean of New School University, however, most university administrators do not appear to feel that the policy of 'admitting students on the basis of their cash value to the University' is a re-

signing matter. There were, after all, no reports of protest resig-
nations at the Irish university which informed academic staff in
2010 that any future academic promotions would be conditional
on academics having actively contributed to the drive to devise
taught post-graduate programmes likely to favour the recruitment of fee-paying students, especially students from overseas.
Indeed, that same Irish university declared in a Strategic Plan
drawn up in 2009 that by 2014 90 per cent of its academic staff
will qualify as being 'research active'. So far, so admirable. However, the definition of 'research active' is based on the fulfilment
of at least one of two explicitly commercial criteria: either winning external research grants or attracting postgraduate tuition
fees, criteria as unrelated to educational value and to the individual employee's academic merit or effort, as they are, in today's
recessionary world, pie in the sky.

THE 'STUDENT EXPERIENCE' INDUSTRY AND THE STANDARDS CRASH

Why should Ireland care about the basis on which universities
choose to appoint, reward, value and promote the academics
staffing Higher Education across the world? Why should we all
be concerned about how the universities charged with the Higher Education of the world's citizens finance themselves? Why
should we be interested in how some US, Australian or British
authors think about the various Higher Education trends and
developments dominating the international landscape today?
Why should we be bothered about the most disparaging account
of contemporary American universities presented by Stanley
Aronowitz, a prolific professor of sociology at the City University
of New York? In a book presenting a litany of complaints about
the system within which he is working, *The Knowledge Factory:
Dismantling the Corporate University and Creating True Higher
Learning* (2001), Aronowitz claims that 'training' has taken the
place of 'higher learning' or 'education' at America's post-sec-

ondary educational institutions. Even in today's top universities, he contends, students are essentially being taught to reproduce received wisdom or knowledge rather than to question or critique it. Aronowitz criticises the US Higher Education system for selling out to corporate America by business-led teaching and by diverting its leading administrators into full-time fundraising.

One very concrete reason why Irish people should care about all these questions is global convergence. This is our future too, and some parts of Irish Higher Education are already living through it. Another is that Aronowitz's complaints are only the tip of the iceberg when it comes to the problem of educational standards in the era of the corporate university. In their book on the topic, *Academically Adrift: Limited Learning on College Campuses*, the two authors, Richard Arum and Josipa Roksa, outline the extent of the collapse in undergraduate academic standards in the US.

> In spite of soaring tuition costs, more and more students go to college every year. A bachelor's degree is now required for entry into a growing number of professions. And some parents begin planning for the expense of sending their kids to college when they're born. Almost everyone strives to go, but almost no one asks the fundamental question posed by *Academically Adrift*: are undergraduates really learning anything once they get there?

Thus reads the blurb of the 'book of the year' on US academia. The authors of *Academically Adrift* quote Harvard's ex-president Derek Bok on the function of the university education. They point out the universal consensus that universities exist to educate students in critical thinking, but they argue that this *raison d'être* is actually betrayed on college campuses the length and breadth of the US.

According to this study, at least 45 per cent of undergraduates failed to demonstrate – following the first two years of college

instruction – any improvement in the three following areas measured by the 'Collegiate Learning Assessment' tool on which the
book's research is based: critical thinking, complex reasoning,
writing skills. Thirty-six per cent of graduates showed no progress in these areas after four years of college. Arum and Roksa
point out that students of mathematics, science, the humanities and social sciences tended to show more progress than those
registered in more directly career-oriented fields like business or
engineering. More progress was also associated with high expectations on the part of instructors making more regular demands
of more reading, writing and thinking from their students. This
finding will not surprise any experienced teacher. However, what
might seem surprising is that the difference made by education
to writing, reasoning and critical skills is almost as disappoint-
ing at the US's elite private four-year institutions as at the public
or even community colleges. As the two authors put it:

> Students are adrift almost everywhere, floating in the
> wreckage of a perfect storm that has transformed higher
> education almost beyond recognition.

And the principal cause of this collapse? According to Arum
and Roksa, it boils down to a deficit in academic commitment
on the part of students. They argue that, upon entering university or college, undergraduates are already 'academically adrift'
and that, once registered in Higher Education, they remain
adrift there. They report a dramatic decline in academic effort
on the part of today's students, citing a decline in the average
time students spent studying. Their surveys show that students
themselves report spending steeply diminished amounts of time
studying relative to those recommended and also relative to
those reported in previous years.

What the authors then point out, however, is that this demonstrable lack of academic focus has not caused any negative
effect on the statistics for the GPA (grade point average, or the

final grade average awarded to students on graduation). They also note preferential enrolment in 'soft' options, where grading is lenient. However, rather than focussing exclusively on the deficit of studious effort on the part of students, the authors of *Academically Adrift* dwell notably on faculty (or academics') accommodation of this decline in standards, and they even point to a tacit, bilateral disengagement contract between student and instructor.

Following these observations the two authors examine the contributory factors to this decline in academic focus across US colleges and universities. They note a general institutional disengagement from academic principles and point as evidence of this to 'the staffing and employment changes implemented in recent decades', that is, the outnumbering of academics by administrators/managers and of tenured by untenured, contingent and therefore vulnerable academic staff.

STUDENTS (ACADEMICALLY) ADRIFT

According to Arum and Roksa, the loss of academic direction in US Higher Education has been caused by poor decisions around academic employment structures and staffing.

> In colleges and universities across the country, not only have part-time instructors increasingly replaced full-time professors, but resources have increasingly been directed towards non-academic functions.

They go on to quote the sociologist Gary Rhoades who has written that over the past three decades non-academic staff have become the fastest growing category of professional employment in US Higher Education.

> While some of these individuals have been hired for administrative functions such as human relations, accounting, and regulatory compliance, Rhoades has observed that the most significant increase has occurred in the

broad area of student services including admissions, financial aid, career placement, counselling, and academic services such as advising and tutoring that have been re-assigned to non-faculty professionals.

In American parlance, 'non-faculty professionals' are non-front-line academics, although the latter too are 'managed professionals' as Gary Rhoades terms them in his book *Managed Professionals: Unionised Faculty and Restructuring Academic Labor* (1998). The authors of *Academically Adrift* observe that the net effect of this development is to elevate the intensity and prominence of non-academic student services, while de-empha-sising role of academics and academic instruction.

On February 20, 2011, Thomas H. Benton, an alias of William Pannapacker (an Associate Professor of English at Hope College, Michigan) published a review of Arum and Roksa's book entitled 'A Perfect Storm in Undergraduate Education'. Benton observes that in his 2010 'State of the Union' address, President Obama included a call for more Americans to go to college in order to make the USA more competitive in a global context. But, as Benton points out, that call is highly problematic.

> [It] raises the question: What good does it do to increase the number of students in college if the ones who are already there are not learning much? Would it not make more sense to improve the quality of education before we increase the quantity of students?

On the question of who or what is responsible for the perceived ineffectiveness of US Higher Education, Benton recognises that politicians and the public are quick to blame academics, but he points out that the latter, 'like all teachers – are working in a context that has been created largely by others'.

Few people outside of higher education understand how little control professors actually have over what students can learn.

In his review of *Academically Adrift*, Benton lists the main reasons for the decimation of standards of academic learning at US universities. Because these don't necessarily speak for themselves, Benton himself elaborates. The list is worth quoting here in full, along with Benton's comments. As we will see in the next section, with one single exception, they apply to the letter within many areas of the Irish Higher Education system. Moreover, they are all systemic and structural, and cannot be blamed on students alone, on academics alone, or on university management alone: they are rather a reflection of our world and our value systems – but a reflection that we prefer to deny.

1. 'Lack of student preparation.' Increasingly, undergraduates are not prepared adequately in any academic area . . . So college professors routinely encounter students who have never written anything more than short answers on exams, who do not read much at all, who lack foundational skills in math and science, yet . . . resist any criticism of their work. . . . Such a combination makes some students nearly unteachable.

2. 'Grade inflation.' It has become difficult to give students honest feedback. . . . As a result, student progress is slowed, sharply. Rubric-driven approaches give the appearance of objectivity but make grading seem like a matter of checklists, which, if completed, must ensure an A. Increasingly, time-pressured college teachers ask themselves, 'What grade will ensure no complaint from the student, or worse, a quasi-legal battle over whether the instructions for an assignment were clear enough?' So, the number of A-range grades keeps going up, and the motivation for students to excel keeps going down.

3. 'Student retention.' As the college-age population de-clines, many tuition-driven institutions struggle to find enough paying customers to balance their budgets. That makes it necessary to recruit even more unprepared stu-dents, who then must be retained, shifting the burden for academic success away from the student and on to the teacher. . . . At some institutions, graduation rates are so high because the academic expectations are so low. Fail-ing a lot of students is a serious risk, financially, for the college and the professor.

4. 'Student evaluations of teachers.' Although a lot of emphasis is placed on research on the tenure track, most faculty members are not on that track and are retained on the basis of what students think of them. The common wisdom, for the untenured, at least – whether it is true or not – is to find ways to keep the students happy . . .

5. 'Enrollment minimums.' Students gravitate to lenient professors and to courses that are reputedly easy, particu-larly in general education. . . . If you are untenured and your courses do not attract enough students, then you can become low-hanging fruit for nonrenewal . . . [so] the curriculum – populated by electives and required courses competing for the lowest expectations – is driven increasingly by student demand rather than by what a community of scholars believes undergraduates should know.

6. 'Lack of uniform expectations.' It is impossible to main-tain high expectations for long unless everyone holds the line in all comparable courses. . . . Faculty members cannot raise expectations by themselves, nor can depart-ments, since they, too, are competing with one another for enrollments.

7. 'Contingent teaching.' Perhaps the most damaging change in higher education in the last few generations

has been the wholesale shift in the composition of the teaching staff. Formerly, full-time, tenured faculty members with terminal degrees and long-term ties to the institution did most of the teaching. Such faculty members not only were free to grade honestly and teach with conviction but also had a deep understanding of the curriculum, their colleagues, and the institutional mission. Now undergraduate teaching relies primarily on graduate students and transient, part-time instructors on short-term contracts who teach at multiple institutions and whose performance is judged almost entirely by student-satisfaction surveys.

8. 'Time constraints.' Contingent faculty members, who are paid so little, routinely teach course loads that are impossible to sustain without cutting a lot of corners. One would think that tenured faculty members, at least, would have the time to focus on student learning, but . . . a growing number of tenured professors [have been turned] into part-time administrators [and] research expectations for tenure-track faculty members have escalated steadily. Teaching becomes a distraction from the activities that are most highly rewarded. The easiest way to save time in the classroom is to limit assignments that require personalised feedback and to give grades that are higher than students expect.

9. 'Curricular chaos.' Many colleges are now so packed with transient teachers, and multitasking faculty-administrators, that it is impossible to maintain some kind of logical development in the sequencing of courses. . . . As a result, some majors have become an almost incoherent grab bag of marketable topics combined with required courses that have no uniform standards. Students are now able to create a path through majors that allows them to avoid obtaining what were once considered essential skills and disciplinary knowledge.

10. 'Demoralised faculty members.' Students may be en-
joying high self-esteem, but college teachers seem to be
suffering from a lack of self-confidence. . . . During the
latest economic crisis – perhaps the endpoint of a 40-year
slide – many of us have felt as if we've become expend-
able, if we are employed at all. That makes it hard for us
to make strong demands on our students . . .

Thomas Benton concludes his article on Arum and Roksa's
book by noting that it points to the failings of an entire system.
As suggested at the outset of this book, there is no conspiracy
at work in global Higher Education. Rather, Higher Education
systems are all determined by much broader social, economic
and political contexts. Arum and Roksa themselves state that all
the accountability systems in the world and even total 'institutional transparency in reporting student academic outcomes'
will not turn back the tide. The factors adding up to 'declining
educational outcomes' are much more complex, and much more
impacted and far-ranging than anything that could 'be dealt
with by the government or educational institutions alone'. Or as
Benton succinctly puts it, 'Education is a billion-dollar tail on
a trillion-dollar dog'. In view of the financial stakes, Arum and
Roksa are themselves 'profoundly skeptical' that students, who
are currently 'empowered as consumers or clients' will place any
value at all on chasing a challenging or fulfilling education, ver-
sus a monetarily promising investment. As Benton says, if this
skepticism is well founded, this can only mean one thing!

[I]t means that our 'failing' system of higher education
actually is working the way it is supposed to, according
to the dictates of the market. The patterns of selection
and resource allocation – and the rising costs of college
education – are not driven by educational needs so much
as they are the result of competition for the most enjoy-
able and least difficult four-year experience, culminating

in a credential that is mostly a signifier of existing class positions.

A further problem plaguing the standards of Higher Education, but not mentioned in Benton's list, is plagiarism or cheating, and it is not limited to student fraud. Occasionally, it bursts onto the public stage in high-profile cases of falsification. Indeed some dramatic examples of the greasy alliance between academia and money or power are provided by various recent scandals. For example, the already mentioned publication of fraudulent research data by a cancer research team in Duke University in the US has been linked, as reported in September 2011 in *The Economist*, to a conflict of interest with two on-campus commercialisation companies. Another high-profile case of academic fraud concerns the German university of Bayreuth, which has been the object of bitter criticism and scrutiny, since it emerged that the German ex-Minister of Defence, Karl Theodor zu Guttenberg, had to resign over revelations that up to eighty per cent of the pages of his doctorate from Bayreuth contained plagiarised passages; when last heard of, the disgraced Minister was facing preliminary criminal proceedings on one hundred counts of plagiarism. The current President of Hungary is also being investigated for having allegedly plagiarised almost 100 per cent of his doctoral thesis from two distant sources. Given the increasing emphasis on the exchange value of academic credits or credentials at the expense of the intrinsic value of academic engagement, the proliferation of such high-profile cases is not really surprising.

No Golden Age, No Utopia

It would be ridiculous to claim that the worldwide cloning of the corporate university model invented the abuse of educational ideals and principles in Higher Education. It did, however, invent their systematic and structural sidelining. Prior to mass education, exclusiveness and elitism were the twin original sins of tertiary education, as access to a university education was largely and inequitably conditional on extreme social privilege. In such circumstances, even their genuine respect for intrinsic academic and educational values was never going to protect Higher Education establishments against (often justified) charges of acting counter to the greater public good. For even when they were fundamentally favourable to such values, universities were clearly associated as a matter of fact with the perpetuation of social privilege, and thereby of inequality and injustice.

The democratisation of a college education can only be celebrated as an unequivocal good as long as within the gates of the university campus the emphasis is on an intrinsically worthwhile and authentic educational experience for all who enrol. Conversely, there is not much progress or value in the blanket provision of a university education unworthy of the name. And this is the risk associated with universities becoming essentially a heavily branded space selling certification rather than defending academic or educational values per se. The signs of this transformation are easy to spot: they include most notably the destruction of the public university, escalating tuition fees, the re-commissioning of academics as sales employees and the creeping blanket fog of managerialist bureaucracy.

Like other universities, the renowned private universities of the US, including the Ivy League schools, open their doors wide to stellar academic (and sporting) talent, regardless of means. Nonetheless, tuition fees are, on the whole, astronomical and rising both in the private US institutions and increasingly in public institutions both in the UK and in the US also, and student and graduate debt is spiralling proportionately. Moreover, student recruitment, especially but not exclusively in the US, is currently the object of intensive gaming rituals. This situation explains the fact that a former Yale administrator can now run a lucrative business advising college applicants on their application strategies, charging them over $35,000 for this service. In such a jungle, it is clear that it will be no easy task for the students themselves to identify, let alone negotiate or critique, the fiercely tenacious social conservatism of Higher Education and its continuing unhealthy relationship with money and power.

In his 2012 book on the US liberal arts education, Andrew Delbanco argues that the US college recruitment system is 'well designed to convince the winners that they deserve their winnings'. Commenting further on the 'culture of elite colleges' in an interview with the e-zine *Inside Higher Education*, Delbanco underlines the fact that, whereas historically an elite college education was at least acknowledged as being due to an accident of moneyed birth, today it seems to be spawning a meritocratic nightmare.

> [It is creating] a self-loving cadre of national leaders, convinced of their superiority to their fellow citizens as measured by tests, income, range of influential 'contacts', and so on.

The testimony of Walter Kirn is telling in this respect. Kirn, an American writer and author of a satirical novel about corporate captivity entitled *Up in the Air* (made into a film of the same name in 2009), tells in his memoir *Lost in the Meritocracy: The Undereducation of an Overachiever* (2009) how a stellar academic trajectory through Princeton left him a coked-up, hollow shell. Although Kirn's father had been a football scholar (to Princeton), he had never been able to perform as a comfortable insider in the corporate world that Princeton had opened up for him. Kirn himself performed superlatively in all his tests and assessments, effortlessly winning an academic scholarship to Princeton. Once ensconced there, he routinely out-performed his peers as an English major and left with a Keasbey scholarship to Oxford. In his own estimation, however, Kirn graduated from Princeton as an over-achieving but 'undereducated' gamer and opinionator, who had never really read his way properly through a single novel. What saved him, in his own view, from a terminally empty existence was, apart from contact with a few academic mentors who believed in him, the library of classics built up via mail order by his mother, a nurse who had taught herself two modern languages in order to read French and Italian masterpieces in the original. Home on vacation, having suffered what he describes as a drug-fuelled mental breakdown, he picked up in a moment of idleness F. Scott Fitzgerald's *The Great Gatsby* from his mother's bookshelves. It was a book he had written essays about at college, but he had never actually 'read' it. Once hooked, he worked his way through his mother's entire library. Kirn's story is a cautionary tale for those who would either look to apparent academic paradises such as the Ivy League universities or to Oxbridge as models of automatic academic integrity. It also cautions against looking back to the sixties or seventies or further back with academic nostalgia. We have already seen that the historical elitism of the moneyed alumni of the top tier American colleges can be seen – by Andrew Delbanco for example – as less pernicious in some respects than that of today's even more smug and blinkered 'meritocracy'.

Kirn himself is not slow, indeed, to point out in an interview that he gave in 2009 about his book with *The Daily Californian* that Ivy League college trajectories failed to prevent graduates from the US's most prestigious universities from dragging the Capitalist West into financial meltdown.

> The very people I went to [Princeton] with – the people who mastered this meritocratic system most assiduously, are the same ones who came to run our kind of financial and governmental establishment. And the qualities of detachment, dishonesty, ambition and indifference that were fostered in these places have now played out on a grand scale to the detriment of tens of millions of people. Citibank, Lehman Brothers, Bear Stearns and all these places are literally staffed by the meritocratic elite. And

look what a damn poor job they did of registering the most basic civic morality in their behavior. I think that there is no greater mark against the system as presently constituted than the fact that its great success stories are the very ones who got us into this awful mess.

Applauding the state university system, especially the public universities of California, Kirn argues that although an 'elite' university education can uphold academic values of critical thoughtfulness, it can also work as indoctrination in groupthink. Thus he recognises that the classes he attended at Princeton did teach him to think critically and independently. Simultaneously, however, the social capital concentrated in Princeton, the herd element, was shoving in the opposite direction, pushing the students to wear the tee-shirt and to identify with a 'class' or caste.

The thing that I couldn't deal with at Princeton also was that here you're being taught in your classes to be skeptical, critical, detached, thoughtful. But socially at the university you're being taught to jump up and cheer with the pack. And not all colleges and universities are quite like that, but a heck of a lot of them are. On the one hand you're being taught to think for yourself, and on the other you're being immersed in groupthink.

3

From Island of Saints and Scholars to Brand Ireland

Irish Higher Education, or Armageddon Delayed

While academia did endure sporadic and isolated collapses from time to time, for example when it went dormant in Fascist Germany or the Soviet Union, what is specific to our age is the global scale of capitulation to essentially the same non-academic – or in some extreme cases – anti-academic agenda. In the United Kingdom, Armageddon began under Thatcher in the early 1990s with Tony Blair's regime finishing off the carpentry on the academic coffin. In his books on UK educational policy, especially *The Education Debate* (2008), Stephen Ball shows how the social, civic and economic meanings of education were collapsed under New Labour into a single obsession with market competitiveness. New Labour based its mantra of education reform on the supposed needs of the globalised 'knowledge economy'. Ball shows that this mantra was broadly congruent with that of the main players in global education policy, the World Bank, the OECD and the WTO, which had long promoted the deregulation of transnational markets.

In terms of policy discourse, if not in practice, Ireland is a relative latecomer to academic Armageddon. The Irish discourse of neo-liberal educational reform only took off in earnest around 2005. Indeed, from the late eighties through to the mid-noughties British colleagues would look in wonder at the greater part of the Irish university system and marvel that academic post-Thatcherism had not crossed the Irish Sea. As the Irish boom took hold it still looked as though things were, in the main, done differently in Irish Higher Education. Around 2005, however, there was a big shift as the country's largest university in particular self-consciously realigned itself, broadly following the US corporate model that Britain too had pile-driven into its Higher Education policy. Some Irish universities rapidly went earlier and further than others – and than most universities in the UK too – in, for example, adopting radically modularised, US-style curricular and degree classification systems, while also copying the UK's version of top-down academic line management. The most striking originality of this Irish reform, though, was that it was pushed through not in adverse, but rather in flourishing, economic circumstances; not so much to save money, as to make more.

To introduce this section on a more positive note, however, in at least two fundamental respects the state of Irish Higher Education is significantly more favourable academically than the one critiqued by certain US and UK insiders as discussed in Section 2. First, tuition fees have been kept relatively low, at least in relation to those two dominant systems, albeit at a very high price for our postgraduates and overseas students. Of course, in the unlikely event that Ireland were to compare its pricing system with that of mainland European systems, in France or Germany, for example, it would appear exorbitant, most especially for non-European students or for postgraduates of all provenances. Second, undergraduates are still, by and large, taught by tenured academics and their interests do not appear to have been sacrificed to the extent that they may have been in parts of the US system: for example, on the altar of the research imperative. It would be tempting to add two other advantages, namely the relatively small scale of the Irish operation and its relatively tardy frogmarch into the corporate swamp. In my experience, however, these are not – or not reliably – protective factors.

As Stephen Ball explains it in his book *The Education Debate*, the UK story of New Labour's education reforms seems to provide the exact script followed belatedly by Ireland's Higher Education policy. Eventually published by the Cabinet Office in 2006, the blueprint, entitled 'The UK Government's Approach to Public Service Reform', emphasizes, according to Ball, principles such as introducing top-down performance management, incentivising greater efficiency and quality of service via full economic costing, and giving users or clients more input into operations. Ball shows the effects of these principles on the roles of parents and students, for example, who are re-configured as consumers. Among the unintended consequences, he identifies a growing disregard for social equity, a lowering of trust, and the marginalisation of meaningful or real educational achievement.

From about 2005, then, certain key institutions within the Irish Higher Education landscape were energetically reconfigured in line with the above-described neo-con, neo-liberal blueprint. Thus, academics in the affected institutions found themselves, to a greater or lesser extent, 'reforming' the administration of their teaching, operating a postgraduate production line, marshalled towards strategic (that is, income-generating) research, growing the research business and, more generally, especially in the current recessionary alarm, directed to bring in the money, regardless of its temperature, any way they can.

PUSHING DISSIDENCE UNDERGROUND

During this time of unparalleled policy change, Irish public discourse on Higher Education was largely confined to media coverage of the views of politicians, state agencies and the most senior university or college administrators/managers. When have coalface practitioners taken to the podium to talk about their work in education as opposed to their area of specialised expertise (economics, technology, energy, art, history, etc.)? Furthermore, on the rare occasions when public discourse on Irish Higher education addresses questions that cannot quite be boiled down to money, the point that is made, again and again, whether by politicians, industrialists, trade unionists or educationalists, concerns the need for Higher Education to foster 'critical thinking'.

Ironically, however, it has been made extremely difficult even for experienced front-line academics to express within or around academia any critical perspective on the Higher Education model imposed through the reforms of recent years, nor on the partially consequential subsidence of academic standards. In an intensely personalised, relatively closed cultural context, one with a history of not standing up very well to authoritarianism or even bullying (from the Catholic hierarchy, for example, or the party whip or – now– the financial markets), it is very difficult to oppose the dominant policy line. Furthermore, the Lilliputian size of Irish Higher Education is not a friend to critical thinking. The better we know the emperor or the emperor's friends, the harder it is to mention the absent clothes.

Clearly, in certain cases, the happy coincidence of real leadership, insight and courage, or of real community and solidarity, either prevented unwise reforms from being pushed through in certain institutions, or mitigated their worst consequences. In other cases, though, the unhappy coincidence of less favourable circumstances has resulted in spectacular losses of academic morale and élan in vast tracts of Irish Higher Education, and in far more serious difficulties too.

In general, where reformed structures and mechanisms, curricular or organisational, were imposed centrally, in a rush and from above rather than from the ground up, they rarely proved enabling. Instead, whatever their intrinsic merits, the manner of their implementation itself militated against benefit. More-over, when open recalcitrance or opposition was dismissed as the reckless attention-seeking of a minority of inflexible mal-contents, critique retreated underground. It may have surfaced as samizdat lampoons, or appeared in anonymous form in blogs, but more typically the unarticulated distress generated disaffec-tion and eventually exit. The losses have been spectacular.

Some decades ago, the ethos one of the two youngest Irish uni-versities, the University of Limerick, under Edward Walsh's pres-idency, was subjected to thoughtful critique in Patricia Palmer's article 'Apples, Arts, Amnesiacs and Emigrants: The University Connection', published in *The Irish Review*. Broadly speaking, however, the ethos of Irish universities was not often so openly critiqued again until the mid-noughties, when the corporate model really took hold across Irish Higher Education. An NUI Maynooth publication entitled *What Price the University*, edit-ed by Thomas Kelly, appeared in 2006 and the reverberations of corporate reform began around the same time to make a definite impact in the Irish media. Although the reporting of the various controversies in *The Irish Times* was not always a model of bal-ance, some of Eddie Holt's columns were remarkable for their lucid analysis of what the Dublin City University academic and journalist liked to call the 'guff' newly surrounding Irish Higher Education. However, without saying why, Holt announced to his readers on one memorable Saturday in 2005 that *The Irish Times* was dispensing with his services. Conversely, the newspaper of record continued to devote several (usually full-page) articles to largely admiring accounts of the 'aims, plans, goals and objec-tives' of the universities, more especially UCD and TCD. Indeed, for some time those universities' press releases would regularly appear in print, largely unchallenged by editorial probing or dis-tance. The most memorable of these concerned the UCD/TCD Innovation Alliance or Academy announced in March 2009. The proud promoters of this engagement promised with straight faces that it would result within ten years in an 'innovation corridor' stretching from Dublin 4 into Dublin 2, a Sili-con strip housing 300 new companies and providing 30,000 new jobs.

In a media development which could only strengthen the sense that Ireland's largest university had a 'special relationship' with the newspaper of record, the glossy PR annual magazine, *UCD Connections* began to be distributed folded into a copy of *The Irish Times*. Despite the departure of Eddie Holt's critical eye, there was also, in fairness, some serious *Irish Times* coverage of Higher Education corporate reform, with two anti-managerialist pieces in particular raising dust. One, published in 2005, was penned by Fintan O'Toole on the basis of an extensive leak from an unnamed UCD academic reportedly too concerned about retaliation – against his discipline and colleagues – to write in his own name. The second, from the newly retired Professor of Politics at UCD, Tom Garvin, was published in 2009. Both ignited relatively long-lived controversies in the Letter Pages of subsequent issues of the newspaper. There were some news controversies as well, in particular the long-lived scandal of the financial details of allegedly unlawful remuneration (the famous incentive bonuses/allowances) investigated by the Dáil's Public Accounts Committee. Yet, all in all, the extent of Ireland's academic Armageddon has remained beneath the public radar. Why?

It is surely not difficult to understand the inertia that takes hold where a culture of compliance has been manufactured. Fear of retaliation is not perhaps the most intimidating consideration, even if it appears to be a real concern given that those academics most trenchant in their opposition to neo-liberal reforms have mostly spoken from retirement. One acting academic who did take the risk of speaking out in the Letter pages of *The Irish Times* explicitly identified the atmosphere in his university as Stalinist in tenor. The totalitarian analogy is not unfounded but there are perhaps far more pressing reasons to hold back than fear of reprisals. For one thing, refusniks have to be prepared to confront and even to alienate not just their employer's praetorian guard but also their own colleagues and even friends. They have to be prepared to be cast as chronic misfits or malcontents, or even as traitors. And to feel or be made feel so uncomfortable and marginalised that they may need to walk away eventually from their job. If they wish to remain in Ireland's particularly 'small world', that probably means walking away from their profession and career as well. There are also, however, more altruistic reasons for academics to hold back. There is the fear of polarising and of thereby weakening a profession or an institution to which they owe much. Or the fear of not being right. Or of having no right to criticise if one doesn't have all the answers. And, of course, the fear of doing more harm than good, the fear of damaging national confidence in Higher Education beyond repair, for example, or of unintentionally harming the lives or livelihoods of people caught up in hoaxes that are not of their making.

There have been exceptions to the deficit of critical debate about the creeping business ethos of Irish Higher Education. Some academics or academic representatives have organised debating, action or information forums within or amongst third-level institutions. One of the most noteworthy and impressive virtual spaces covering discussion of the issues affecting contemporary Higher Education is an Irish website called Ninth-Level Ireland. The name, which is a reference to the ninth level of Hell, speaks for itself. Even on this site, however, what is remarkable, in addition to the thoroughness of its English-language press-watch and blog-alert on issues critical to Higher Education, is the relative paucity of signed online commentary on, or discussion of, the issues. Although former DCU president Ferdinand von Prondzynski's blog is a prolific exception, many contributors to frank online discussions seem reluctant to speak in their own name. Indeed, the prevalent use of aliases in Ninth Level Ireland's relatively short discussion threads speaks volumes about the culture of constraint within the sector.

Campus Business I: Academic Subsidence

So what could academics have been risking their jobs to expose or oppose over the past seven or eight years? Top of the list has to be the educational fall-out of the business reform playing out in Irish Higher Education. How did it happen that so many Irish colleges and universities turned their students into clients and consumers? Why are academic standards and values nose-diving? And have these questions anything to do with the hustling that currently passes for Higher Education policy? Are they related to the wagon-circling reforms that have already been put in place in order to bolster a more business-like image for Higher Education across the board? How, in concrete terms, have things come to this pass?

Curricular Reform: Commercialist Gimmickry?

In a star-struck system determined to take US Higher Education as its business model, it was always going to be a mere matter of time before the US mantra of curricular flexibility would be copied. This would be achieved by implementing a more or less radical programme of 'modularisation', with a new emphasis on flexibility of degree programmes or interdisciplinarity.

In a recent posting on the electronic publication, the *Huffington Post*, Wesleyan University President Michael Roth popped up to argue very strongly against 'the abolition of departments'. Roth makes the fairly elementary point that 'it doesn't make sense to call for cross-disciplinary programs if there are no disciplines'. In other words, core subjects and skills have to be maintained and taught as such.

> [F]rom language training to quantitative competency, there are skills that can't be suddenly wished into existence when it comes time to share them with collaborators.

Without going into technicalities, it is important to recognise that structural university reforms such as modularisation or rationalisation (the abolition of subjects or departments – usually amalgamated or 'disappeared' into larger multi-subject, would-be interdisciplinary units called cost-centres) have meant and still mean very different things in different Higher Education systems, in different institutions and in different academic areas. There is a world of difference, for example, between the more radical modularisation systems, on the one hand, and on the other the 'modularisation-lite' that involves little more than re-branding traditional courses with a module barcode. What is essential to understand, however, is the connection between three phenomena: first, the structural university reforms that are being challenged in this book; second, the commercial or corporate agenda driving these reforms; and third, the fall in standards of core educational aspiration and attainment.

Although modularisation has an academic rationale in that it enables curricular and interdisciplinary flexibility, its principal rationale is plainly commercial in nature. Indeed, long before some Irish universities adopted modularisation across the board, they were already offering 'modular degrees' which worked extremely well. These were evening degrees taken in a more flexible structure by 'non-standard' or 'mature' students who, in contrast to 'day students', paid significant tuition fees. The salient point is that modularisation enables universities to market themselves to a very diverse clientele, including atypical students (non-school leavers), on a fee-per-module basis. Indeed, the particular attraction (both for vendor and client) is this flexible pricing structure. The 'modular' evening degree was usually, however, modular in name only. While the 'modular' students may have had to choose between fewer options than the 'non-modular' day students, the same programme was broadly followed by all students of a given subject. For the very able and very focussed student, 'real' or even 'radical' modularisation may be beneficial. But for the average undergraduate and for certain disciplines, there can be considerable difficulties in ensuring that the course of study is coherent and that it ensures progression from one level to the next in the core subjects or 'majors'. Hence, modularisation carries the risk of a fragmented 'education' where all semblance of integration or progression is indefinitely deferred. Certainly, degree programmes can be too sealed-off, too closed up. But equally, modularisation can prove an immense challenge to the integrity and to the balance of thoughtful programmes of study put together over decades of trial and error. The big casualties of curricular fragmentation are, inevitably, detail and depth. To explain why, we could look at the Booker prize-winning novel, *The Finkler Question* by Howard Jacobson, which offers the following caricature of the curricular consumerism that has taken over parts of Irish Higher Education.

> He'd been a modular, bits-and-pieces man at university, not studying anything recognisable as a subject but fitting components of different arts-related disciplines, not to say indisciplines, together like Lego pieces. Archaeology, Concrete Poetry, Media and Communications, Festival and Theatre Administration, Comparative Religion, Stage Set and Design, the Russian Short Story, Politics and Gender. On finishing his studies – and it was never entirely clear when and whether he had finished his studies, on account of no one at the university being certain how many modules made a totality – Treslove found himself with a degree so unspecific that all he could do with it was accept a graduate traineeship at the BBC.

Jacobson is exaggerating, of course, but we have already seen how the US 'student experience industry' has been criticised from within for under-playing the studious input required from students. And we also saw that the risk of under-input was greatest where students could avoid any real or challenging engagement with the scope, detail and depth of specific disciplines. In some Irish Higher Education contexts, the modular chickens are already coming home to roost.

The problem is at its most severe in those unfortunate institutions where academics have had to contend with the promotion of a particularly shallow kind of educational gimmickry. Even educationally astute commentators are not always completely alive to the implications of this danger. For example, in an interview with a student newspaper at one Irish university, the then Minister of Education is quoted as having declared that she 'loved' the curricular innovations that were now allowing students 'to dabble in subjects outside their area'. The former Minister's praise, which lives on, as we will see, in the current Minister's apparent affection for interdisciplinarity, inadvertently identifies the chief difficulty inherent in radical modularisation models: namely, the risk of transforming at least the first year of Higher Education, and possibly even subsequent years too, into a cross between a Higher 'transition year' and an academic Club Med. The problem is not so much that whereas the Celtic Tiger was kind to Higher Education dabblers and dilettantes, the Global Dragon will be merciless. It is rather that the dabbler mentality irreversibly and absolutely confirms our students' status as consumers, sampling their way through the college hypermarket.

Just because modularisation was introduced in certain Irish universities as a rather brash commercial packaging of the Irish Higher Education product does not mean that it is automatically anti-educational. And just because simultaneously radical and idiosyncratic versions were imposed in some institutions at a time when Higher Education standards were already starting to drop, and just because they were imposed from the top down and without adequate planning and consultation, does not mean that modularisation is an inherently anti-academic model. It remains, however, that while modularisation has presented a whole new set of risks and difficulties, it is quite unclear which large-scale specifically academic or educational problems it has 'fixed' – with the possible exception of over-specialisation. But does that really count as a problem? Some would say, after all, that the purpose of Higher Education is at least partly to provide specialisation in a given discipline.

Marketing the Student Experience

In today's saturated Higher Education market, a college administration's success is measured by the numbers of students who select its courses as their CAO 'first choice'. Colleges are, as we know from aggressive prime-time radio advertising, vying with one another to attract students to their product: their friendly staff, their campus experience, the promised buying power of their qualifications. The fact is, though, that anything that risks minimising students' perception of the sheer effort required of them in order to benefit from an academic education of any real value is unfortunate in the extreme. Any salesmanship that creates an impression among students that they can somehow 'get' a proper 'university education' without a certain level of academic ability, motivation and commitment and some very hard work is not just misleading; it is irresponsible. Any system that allows or encourages 'dabbling', or that can be interpreted as allowing students to combine a certain number of easier core modules and easy elective modules in non-core subjects as the 'smart' way to get a degree, will further encourage a shopping-trolley approach to education and will, in the long run, make it impossible for academics to reach many, if not most, of their students other than as consumers. All too often, a misplaced emphasis on the improvement of academics' teaching performance is part of this consumerist approach to education, because the idea behind it is to improve the 'shopper' experience. The teacher's role is thus overplayed, and because the student experience is reduced to one of passive consumption, the true relation between the student's own effort and achievement is distorted and he or she is ultimately deceived and disempowered.

In relation to the enhancement of the campus experience, although Irish universities do now offer sports scholarships and although they have invested enormously in campus facilities, they cannot be accused of deserting the core academic mission for 'campus experience enhancement' in the manner of certain American universities. Naturally, the promise of a socially and culturally vibrant campus helps to recruit students to a given institution. If, however, it is not clear to students that participation in the social, cultural or civic life of the university or college is its own reward, and if, in order to encourage such participation, it is felt necessary to signal formal recognition of such input in a student's graduation transcript, then that is regrettable even if it is justifiable in a circular sort of way. The problem is that promotion of the 'campus experience', unless very carefully handled, risks further blurring the place of real academic endeavour in Higher Education. If, for example, participation in a non-academic campus event, such as a fashion show, a musical or a talent competition, gives students any academic advantage, such as 'homework passes' or deadline extensions on academic submissions, or if the university administration characterises such participation as 'college business' excusing students from class attendance, this will surely end up confusing all involved about the real priorities of Higher Education.

Declining to Classify

The introduction of radically modularised systems usually comes with substantive changes in the way a graduate's academic attainment is assessed and expressed. In a degree programme centred on two 'major' disciplines – for example, Italian and history or mathematics and economics – graduates from the most extremely modularised Irish universities are typically awarded not a degree result classified for each subject (1st class honours in maths, upper 2nd class honours in French, for example), but rather a global, averaged result for all the modules taken, including elective modules from outside their major discipline(s). This is called the grade point average (the GPA). As previously, students will receive a transcript of their final grade for each module (or course element) that they studied, but unlike before, there can be no summative identification of the overall standard reached within their chosen disciplines. In traditional degree classification systems, that overall summative standard of attainment in individual disciplines is agreed at an exam board meeting in consultation with all the teachers who would have tracked the student's progress over at least three years and in consultation with external examiners qualified to comment on the national or (preferably, of course) international comparability of the overall standards being applied and on the overall weighting of different course elements.

It is difficult to see how the function of a degree as a clear guarantee of the coherence, integrity and level of a student's attainment in a specific discipline would not be undermined by the move to merely arithmetical averaging. After all, very close reading of the actual composition of each graduate's list of modules will be required in order for employers to assess the overall level of attainment within a given discipline. Indeed, with interdisciplinary modules all the rage, even the simple exercise of counting the number of modules falling within a particular discipline becomes a challenge in itself. Secondary schools seeking to recruit teachers, for example, will be challenged to figure out just what standard was achieved in the core subject(s) which the graduate will be asked to teach. This reduced reliability or legibility of 'modular credits' as a measure of a graduate's grasp of the 'nucleus' of a given subject or discipline is not the only threat to academic standards in Ireland's educational continuum.

There is also the danger that Irish institutions may follow some international trends which favour the inclusion of 'credits' for involvement in non-academic campus social life such as sport clubs and/or for off-campus, non-academic 'work experience'.

Doubtlessly some Irish colleges or universities have not seen fit to dispense with the toil of 'traditional', endlessly deliberative examination boards; nor to cut costs by restricting their nomination of external examiners or peer reviewers to those working on the small island of Ireland; or to move from classified degrees to the GPA system. This is not surprising, given that this system is still in pilot mode in UK Higher Education. Indeed, the fact that British institutions are advancing only slowly towards grade averaging and against some well-informed resistance, gives some measure of the inexplicable precipitation with which this change was imposed at one fell swoop by certain Irish university administrations. Whether students, academics or the wider society look on that reform as educational progress or regression, three things are sure. One: the lifting of the obligation to award to students a definite, undiluted overall degree result in a distinct discipline (with due regard for the fact that not all courses or modules are of equal weight or importance), removes from the academic profession one of the most time-consuming and stressful deliberative decisions that we used to have to make collegially, as discipline-specific teams. As anyone confronted with the inevitable yearly degree-level exam meetings will confirm, these marathons could always be relied upon to trigger the most uniquely painful of work-related migraines. Two: the GPA system relieves academics of much of the double responsibility of maintaining core academic standards in their discipline as a whole while attempting to do justice to students' efforts, progress and achievement. In fact, it neatly disguises the mechanics of grade inflation by replacing the ultimate collegial judgement call by a purely arithmetic averaging exercise performed by migraine-immune calculators. Three: in displacing the onus of interpreting a set of grades in a given discipline onto future employers or post-graduate course directors, this reform doesn't so much kick the grading can down the road as puck it into a deep, dark drain. *Cui bono?*

Assessment-led Learning

More radical modularisation models usually require academic staff to be as creative and inventive as possible in designing flexible 'assessment suites' for measuring 'learning outcomes'. This typically implies a vastly increased emphasis on continuous assessment, especially student-directed projects, essays or reports. Since there have been suggestions to introduce more project-based assessment into second-level Irish education, it needs to be pointed out that, although this policy change has its fans, it has run into some very serious problems at third level. The biggest challenge posed is perhaps that of rampant cheating and plagiarism. Cyber-plagiarism (from the internet) or simple copying from another student's assignment are relatively easy to detect once students submit their work electronically, However, it is still impossible to be certain that work not done in supervised conditions is the student's own work and not that of some 'helper'. But that only really leaves the option of regular secure testing within the twelve-week semester, an option that amounts, however, to a most oppressive regime of constant evaluation, with little or no time for reflective thinking.

Absenteeism: The Deserted Campus

Inevitably, the general cultural intensification of online communication has been embraced by Higher Education, both for better and for worse. It involves such minor administrative changes as online choice of, and registration to, courses described in online 'module descriptors', as well as more substantive educational changes such as exclusively online submission of work, online communication with instructors and online submission of feedback on courses.

Despite the innumerable benefits of this cultural change, certain difficulties are arising. For example, online administration of learning appears to reduce the students' sense of having a physical, departmental home in the university. It erodes their face-to-face familiarity with the academic and academic support staff who work there. More dramatically, this dilution of direct contact may well be linked to an apparent reduction of our students' sense of the importance of 'being there', or of 'turning up' (to class). Despite increasingly desperate efforts to counter the trend of low attendance (for example, spot tests or awarding up to 30 per cent module credit for attendance/participation in class), the problem has inexplicably continued beyond the boom into the dog-days of the recession. The fact is that face-to-face interaction of academics with students and of students with each other is severely reduced by the 'remote control' administrative model. The impact of absenteeism on 'unmeasured' or 'unmeasurable' outcomes – such as the ability to discuss, debate or question academic matters – is probably very significant. Unfortunately, student absenteeism affects not just the academic standards attained by the absentees; it also depresses the general level of enthusiasm, participation, engagement and resonance for those students who do turn up prepared to engage.

It would be difficult to put into words the effect of student absenteeism on campus culture. It appears to have taken some college administrations as much by surprise as did the Irish economy's crash-landing in 2008. After all, in 2004 one administration promised that its reforms would issue in a 24/7 campus. Yet, even before cost-saving measures forced effective campus shut-down at weekends even during term-time, some building managers were reportedly confronted at Christmas 2007 with an end-of-term toilet-paper mountain, so unexpected and dramatic had been post-reform reduction in campus footfall.

Student-Teacher Dynamics in a Low-Trust Culture

As already mentioned, academics are increasingly confronted, in Ireland as elsewhere, with plagiarism and other types of academic fraud. Real as these issues are, and relevant as they are to the deficit of trust within academia, they are at least widely acknowledged as such and are being tackled. There is also, however, a definite trend – in certain Irish Higher Education institutions at least – towards the undermining of students' trust in the educational role of academics. Some of that undermining is without doubt inadvertent, an unintended by-product of well-meant efforts from within Higher Education itself to improve the 'student experience'. It is, however, most confusing for students and most demoralising for their teachers. It can be seen at work in its less benign form in such phenomena as 'rate-my-teacher' charts or in the 'teacher-bashing' punditry that is such a feature of populist political pressure on second-level education. It can happen, and has happened, that certain forces of darkness within Higher Education itself exacerbate this trend. Distrust can thus be created or manipulated in the service of political or business interests that are only too happy to encourage students to think of themselves as consumers. The problem is that consumer rights and academic or educational principles often, of course, collide.

The enthusiastic embrace by university administrations of student feedback mechanisms is an obvious pressure point in this respect. In a high-trust culture, and presumably some of Ireland's Higher Education institutions do operate in such a culture, the process of teaching feedback should do nothing but enhance – on both sides indeed – the self-reflective, self-realising enrichment enabled by the educational relationship. In such a culture, however, feedback would not be solicited or processed by third parties. Instead, teachers would collect it directly (though anonymously) from their students, preferably before the course is already over. Conversely, where teaching/learning feedback is organised online and centrally at the end of each module, instead of encouraging critical self-questioning or creative endeavour on the part of teachers, it can potentially lead instead to a mutually self-protective, risk-averse shutdown.

Remote feedback presents other problems too. For example, whereas few students will refuse to give anonymous feedback directly to their tutors or teachers, they may fail to offer online feedback in sufficient numbers for it to be really useful. At present, the average completion rate for online centralised feedback in at least one Irish university is understood to be about 35 per cent. This is not, of course, statistically reliable, at least in courses that were well-attended. In some cases, though, that percentage might correspond quite accurately to the percentage of students with full attendance records (although it is rarely admitted, abysmal levels of attendance are not rare, especially in first- and second-year undergraduate courses). But in such a scenario, the teaching feedback exercise is almost an irrelevance, compared to the problem of student absenteeism.

The Risk of Contagion

One of the main reasons why it is so important to recognise the unintended consequences of some of the mad-cap reforms road-tested in certain Irish universities over recent years is that some of them are still being hailed in Irish public discourse as 'the way to go', not just for other colleges but also for the second-level system. The crucial question to be asked of any educational reform is surely whether or not it will help to reinforce not so much the exchange value as the intrinsic value of education. All around us systems of exchange value are wobbling or collapsing. And whenever exchange values fall – the financial or monetary value of a painting or a house or a diploma on the market, for example – then intrinsic value starts to matter more (again). In other words, society as a whole has to start to think again of education as an end in itself, and not just, or not exclusively, as a means to an end.

Partly in recognition of this truth, it has become common-place lately to emphasise the importance of developing critical thinking even at second level. This emphasis is often accompa-nied by a condemnation of rote learning and terminal examina-tions. The risk is, of course, to expect pupils or students to have innovative or critical opinions on things about which they are only superficially or patchily knowledgeable. There is certainly a difference between deep understanding and searching analysis on the one hand, and learning by heart on the other. But in any discipline a sound mental substratum of first principles has to be in place before any higher order thinking can take place. In oth-er words, students of chemistry need to know and understand the periodic table, students of languages need to internalise the sound system and the structural or grammatical system of the language they are studying. Some memorisation is essential therefore, along with an understanding of the principles under-lying what has to be known off by heart. Project work may lessen the abuse of passive learning but the proliferation of assessment by project work is not necessarily a positive if the baby of the 'crucial substratum of learning' is chucked out with the bathwa-ter of 'parroting without understanding'. Especially if the issue of cheating has not been properly addressed.

Academic Standards Adrift?

The previous section of this book featured a list of factors held by some to militate in the US against undergraduate educational standards. All of these, with one exception, have been causing standards to 'decline by degrees' in Irish Higher Education as well. It is worth recalling once more the factors blamed in the US with leading directly to falling standards, this time with specific comment on the Irish context.

Lack of Student Preparation

Irish students do not seem to enter college with an inflated sense of their own abilities. The problem is probably not, moreover, that Irish undergraduates do not have opinions or that they are reluctant to express these. It seems to be, rather, that so many school-leavers underestimate the level of real attainment, interest, motivation and understanding needed in order to make real progress in a given discipline at third level. Arguably, it is the job of Higher Education to help third-level students to develop critical thinking and to understand that the real academic challenge is not so much to know the right answer, but to be able to think of the 'right' or the 'real' questions.

It seems that the difficulty now for Irish Higher Education is less that incoming students have underdeveloped or non-existent skills in critical thinking, than that far too many of them are academically unreachable because of their inability to focus on precise detail or to concentrate on real depth. 'Critical thinking' is what academics are there to model for students. It is surely what we are paid to do, to transmit, to encourage, to develop and, in so far as it can be taught, to teach. But student inability to appreciate or grasp detail and a lack of interest in depth are really serious problems. Not for academics. In fact, all vocational academics will automatically try to take students forward from whatever academic level they seem to be at. That is our job. No, the problem is, rather, that it is extremely difficult for those students who *do* have a high level of academic attainment and aspiration to tolerate the level at which third-level teaching then has to be pitched. And this is a problem for society as a whole, because it means a general dampening or 'dumbing down' of (supposedly) Higher educational standards.

It is true that, more generally, university teachers have their work cut out for them in trying to explain even to very able students why it is not really enough to work in two terminally accelerated 13-week bursts, corresponding to the two academic semesters, thereby 'neatly parking' their study into less than half a year. This, of course, is nothing new. However, what is new is that, whenever there is critical discussion of the challenges facing Higher Education, one increasingly frequent reflex reaction is to suggest that formal term-time or class-contact hours should be extended. In fact, though, it is not instruction-time that should be increased, but rather private study-time. Again, the salient point is that active, extra and intense academic preparation and engagement *on the part of the students themselves* is the only effective and empowering investment ultimately.

Grade Inflation

Ireland may not have reached the point of private universities and colleges in the US where the average grade has reportedly risen from C+ twenty years ago to A- today, or even the point of UK universities, where 80 per cent of classified degree results reportedly fall into the 1st or Upper 2nd brackets. In fact, however, whether we consider 'class of degree', grade point average or grade point sum, all academic credit systems or currencies are gradually being degraded to the point where it is not the degree that counts, but the university awarding the degree, or at least how selective that university is in admitting students. Meanwhile, the pressure on academics to award high(er) grades for individual modules, assignments etc. seems to be increasing all the time. E-mail correspondence contesting grades is becoming the norm as are requirements to explain exactly which boxes must be ticked on a given assignment for it to merit an A grade.

Student Retention Pressure

Retention is a concern for university administrations in Ireland as in other public systems of Higher Education. This is because state funding is set to follow not just numbers of students registered, but also the numbers graduating. As a consequence of this, it is increasingly difficult, administratively, for academics to indicate that students have failed to meet a satisfactory standard in a given course. In general, they must execute carefully orchestrated acrobatics if they wish to override the system's gravitation towards passing grades (by compensation across modules) and in order to ensure that students who graduate with degrees meet certain minimal standards in core subjects. One big concern would be that internalised administrative pressure to retain students will eventually overcome all residual academic resistance.

Student Evaluation of Teaching

As already acknowledged, formal, anonymous feedback from students, whether positive, negative or neutral, can be very helpful to academics in pitching and fine-tuning their teaching. Documentary evidence of the use of such formal feedback mechanisms by academics has indeed formed part and parcel of academic promotions for at least twelve years in my experience. For all the reasons outlined above, however, indirect feedback processes, implemented and monitored by university administrations, raise serious questions.

Enrolment Minimums and Culture of Low Expectations

Colleges will not usually be willing to run subjects which attract too few students and those falling foul of enrolment minimums are usually those that appear to make too many demands on students. This is the case everywhere and not just in Ireland. It eventually leads to a culture where any teacher anxious not to become redundant will tailor their courses to student expectations. Whether that is a good thing or a bad thing depends on where one is standing. But certainly, the fact is that in radically modularised systems, course descriptions will typically be reviewed and 'approved' by various executive committees before 'going live'. The resulting standardised expression of 'learning outcomes' and 'module delivery details' often make for deadening reading. In other words, if 'greater expectations' sneak back in during 'module delivery' it will be despite the bureaucratisation of module quality 'command and control' and not because of it.

Contingent Teaching

In statistical terms the contract permanency of Ireland's Higher Education teaching staff is currently favourable compared with the US picture. However, if the principle of tenure is threatened, then this relatively favourable situation will not continue.

Inadequate Administrative Support for Academics

It can happen that, tenured or untenured, academics working in the less cherished disciplines in the Irish corporate university are deprived of adequate administrative support. In certain respects, academics have always done a certain amount of administration (inputting, maintaining and retrieving student data, for example), but it seems strange that, even at the height of the Irish boom, a lecturer responsible for the academic coordination of certain (loss-making) disciplines involving up to fifteen full-time academic staff would be required to manage this coordinating role in addition to the rest of their own academic and administrative duties, without any administrative support. Especially when, pre-reform, there would have been at least one senior administrator allocated to the support of students and staff within that discipline. Such examples of 'rationalisation' and de-skilling speak volumes about the shift in priorities within the corporate university from 'academic work' to 'administration'.

Curricular Chaos

Academics and administrators in Irish Higher Education do their best to ensure that graduating students have acquired the essential skills and disciplinary knowledge appropriate to the qualification that they receive. However, as with the corporate university's curricular drive towards interdisciplinarity, the logical corollary of the fragmentation inherent in a 'pick 'n mix' approach to education is 'hit 'n miss' coverage of what would normally be regarded as the core curriculum of a given discipline. In recessionary times, as retiring academic staff are no longer being replaced in non-profitable disciplines, academic coverage is bound to become even more 'miss' than 'hit'.

Demoralised Academics: In Ireland Too?

As we will see, where the Irish boom coincided with an extensive and rapid embedding of the corporate model within Irish universities, this was associated with elevated levels of demoralisation and alienation amongst academics. Predictably, there are no indications, thus far anyway, that the crash-landing of the boom is doing much to lift already depressed morales.

CAMPUS BUSINESS II: TIPPING THE BALANCE TOWARDS ADMINISTRATION

As we have seen, the extremely demanding tenure conditions prevailing in US Higher Education system have required academics to devote their energies principally to individual research or scholarship. This policy appears to have encouraged the widespread delegation of undergraduate teaching to untenured and/ or non-tenure track instructors, who are often in no position to call into question policies such as the application of admission, throughput or output targets.

Far from this particular affliction dominating Irish Higher Education, in some institutions at least there has been what could almost be seen as a reverse movement which, unfortunately, has not been wholly positive in its effects on academic standards. Put briefly, vast amounts of managerialist energy have been directed in some Irish universities at focussing sustained attention on the teaching skills of academic staff. If sub-par teaching skills in Irish Higher Education were a serious problem, this might be a welcome trend. However, as we have just seen, it is likely that many of the chief causes of declining Higher Educational standards lie elsewhere. As part of this sometimes misplaced focus on improving the teaching skills of academics, there have been two drives which have not had an entirely positive impact. The first is the aggressive and intensive development of 'taught Masters' courses, which are comparatively lucrative (because, of course, full tuition fees are charged even to domestic postgraduate students), and an accentuation of the 'taught' element of PhD 'programmes' (again, presumably, to justify rather extortionate fees). The overall effect of this development, apart from justifying elevated fee income, is to emphasise 'teaching' at the expense of 'research'. Above all, it reduces demands on the research student, transferring them instead to the teacher. In this way, the positioning of the student as (re)searcher, that is, as the person who plays an active role in imagining the questions as well as in searching for the answers, is deferred or postponed. The second questionable trend consists in an attempt to measure and to reward the direct or indirect impact of scholarship or research on teaching. The effect of both trends is to limit research by directing it ever more towards teaching and the same drift occurs when universities only encourage research that 'fits in' with the research areas defined as expedient or strategic in five-year plans.

In general, of course, the raising of pedagogical consciousness within Higher Education must be regarded as a positive development. Moreover, intense, coordinated and proactive attention is incontestably required in order to face the many challenges presented by teaching in Higher Education., These include perennial problems such as those linked to assessment (cheating/plagiarism, over-assessment, under-assessment, timing of assessments, grade inflation, and so on), but also to standards (how to maintain student enrollment numbers and graduation rates without dropping standards to unacceptable levels).

It would be unfair not to acknowledge the work of the administrative taskforces dedicated within Irish Higher Education to identifying and meeting these and other pedagogical challenges. Equally, however, it would be pointless to deny that, however constructively meant, administration-led policies to 'improve teaching' sometimes run the risk of undermining the specificity of academic values. It is a well-kept secret that a major part of the current (policy-driven, that is, state- or government-directed) effort to 'improve' teaching and learning at third level is actually a response to the sheer magnitude and extent of problems that have presented as unforeseen consequences of ill-judged research-promoting reforms introduced in the very recent past at great speed and without adequate planning. Furthermore, this whole débâcle shows that too much administrative or managerial emphasis on the performance of teaching and assessment risks pandering, in some instances at least, to the illusion that increased quality-management of teaching or even 'better teaching' will, in and of itself, correct problems that are in reality of quite a different scale. For example, it is well recognised that interactive small-group teaching is generally more effective than large-group, non-interactive lectures. However, if the students enrolled in small groups include significant proportions of absentees or students at a serious academic disadvantage in terms of their level of basic academic competency, then far too few students will benefit from one of the main benefits of a college education: namely, interactive learning from/with peers. No amount of 'teaching management' or 'teaching improvement' is going to square that circle.

In other words, unless or until society at large faces up to the implications of the vicious circle of the automatic, transmission-belt misdirection of all, even the academically disinterested or unprepared, into an academic education, a majority of registered students will lack the necessary motivation to study. Instead they will continue to believe, as they are indeed encouraged to, that getting 'credits' for their degrees means what 'credit' means in daily life – get it now and pay later (if at all). Real students are students who are motivated to study, and of course no expense or effort should be spared in ensuring that their study is enabled by pedagogically-aware academics. But nothing, not even the extraordinary effort being poured into improving the 'student experience' of both teaching and assessment at college, will do anything other than reinforce the culture which either explicitly or implicitly views Higher Education essentially as a purchase agreement between a customer and a service provider, and which instrumentalises academics and commodifies knowledge to that end.

Hardwiring the Managerialist Model

It would seem that cash-strapped governments the world over broadly favour the corporate Higher Education model. And from the policy statements emanating from the Irish government, including the broadly supportive statements about private for-profit Higher Education provision, we can infer that Ireland is no exception.

The corporate university is typically based on a tripartite academic structure, corresponding to its three main (academic) income streams: research, undergraduate studies, and postgraduate studies. At its most bureaucratic, this system means that every faculty, every school or section, and every subject, department or discipline has its head of research, its head of teaching and learning, and its head of postgraduate studies. The restructuring of Higher Education along the separated lines of research, teaching and graduate studies replaced a more holistic organisation with teams of discipline-specific academics coordinated by one elected head, *primus inter pares*. This may appear to be a very small, technical adjustment, but its consequences can be immense. It means, for example, a proliferation of management roles and a compartmentalisation of the individual academic's research, teaching and mentoring roles. Above all, it puts the emphasis on an artificial structure instead of affirming the holistic and complex nature of the integrated life (scholarship, research, undergraduate and postgraduate studies) of a given discipline or a given academic within the overall university.

On paper, this homogenising, top-down transmission of policies from super-ordinate (university and college or faculty) to subordinate (school or subject) 'heads' and 'committees' might look very tidy and pleasing, but in practice, it diverts huge amounts of academic energy into bureaucracy. For reasons that often prove difficult to explain to disbelieving academic insiders, let alone to outsiders, managerialism erodes academic integrity and identity by imposing superfluous layers of superordinate management and by emphasising administrative structures at the expense of academic subjects or fields. Thus, when they are dealing with bigger academic units such as multi-subject schools instead of with a particular department centred on their specific subject, the students of that subject will typically have a reduced sense of having a distinct home or port of call on campus. Moreover, an extra layer of academic administration is thereby created, with attendant costs. This is because each individual subject or discipline will still have its own head, and if it is large enough, its own 'teaching and learning' officer, 'research officer', and so on. However, in parallel, individual subjects may lose their own dedicated administrative support personnel, resulting in academics doing most if not all academic administration themselves (student data inputting and maintenance, answering students' administrative queries, etc). Worse still, several academics from the various individual subjects will necessarily be diverted from their core academic activities within those subjects into purely administrative roles serving a new layer of' 'supra-departmental' or supra-disciplinary management, a layer with no academic *raison d'être*. For every academic sucked into such 'make work' on the executive of the newly created superordinate structure, there is a whole cohort of students who will inevitably lose out on close, subject-specific academic attention. In addition, the range of academic courses on offer to students will necessarily be reduced relative to what it would be if academics diverted into management had more time to work on their teaching or scholarship.

Again, to a layperson, this reform will appear to be very technical and obscure, but its significance will not be lost on the vocational academic or indeed on other managed professionals: its principal – possibly unintended but incalculably damaging – consequence is academic asset-stripping.

Blind Faith in Structures and Processes

The word 'bureaucracy' comes from the French *bureau*, meaning office. Bureaucracies are run by an officer class, and they emphasise structures and processes rather than work, and recognise offices and office-holders rather than individual faces. They work superbly well in armies, for example, where large numbers of foot-soldiers must follow orders without question. The corporate university is heavily bureaucratised. Thus, even though some Irish corporate universities misleadingly re-named their various faculties (Arts, Medicine, etc.) as 'colleges', these structures are *not run collegially*, but are rather managed by a vertical chain of command centred on executive committees. As a result, plenary meetings of 'college' academics are mostly non-events, largely taken up by reports from the executive (the heads of research, teaching/learning, and postgraduate studies). The result is often a deficit of open and multilateral debate on broad policy issues. Furthermore, there is a sense that such debate as may take place is largely futile since it is unlikely to be fed back into the organisation's rigid executive pyramid. Meetings of academics then come to resemble managerial reporting sessions rather than a forum for real exchange. And naturally this deficit of substantive and meaningful interaction is reflected in attendance levels. In one Irish university, the conversion of the role of 'faculty meetings' into that of top-down reporting sessions was underlined by the highly symbolic demolition of faculty meeting-rooms in

2005. The erstwhile meeting rooms were reconstructed into a set of vice-presidential suites, with the result that plenary faculty meetings of academic staff had to take place in classrooms, with the various executive officers seated at the head of the class, reading out their reports to ever-dwindling audiences.

Campus Business III: Competitive Trading

Not only do the individual Institutes of Technology and the individual universities have different cultures from one to the other, but the mission and culture of the Institutes, while related to those of the universities, are quite different in some respects. It is worth repeating the chief caveat expressed in the preface to this book, namely that academic Armageddon has probably affected different areas of Irish Higher Education in very different ways and to very different extents. It is also worth adding that, while it would probably be an impoverishment for Irish Higher Education were the Institutes to betray their specificity, it would be an outright calamity if they were to repeat, in so doing, the irreversible educational blunders made by some of the more corporate universities.

It is no secret that, while newer Irish universities such as University of Limerick and Dublin City University may have followed some corporate trends earlier than the more traditional universities, and while they may even exemplify these trends more deeply and more fully, the corporatisation of Ireland's traditional universities has been a uniquely destructive process. The relatively long institutional history of such universities meant that, when invasive structural surgery was performed, it caused a definitive historical rupture with a previous order that had evolved over many decades or even centuries. So, while they are not necessarily the best/worst examples of the Irish corporate university model, they are distinguished by the take-no-prisoners brutality of their corporate make-overs. As with most cultural revolutions, it was not, of course, a case of *Paradise Lost*, but the more 'corporate afterwards' did not, in most respects, favourably compare with the more 'collegiate beforehand'.

In their mindful book, *Saving Education in the Age of Money*, James Engell and Anthony Dangerfield refer to the contemporary 'imperative to move ahead as fast as possible'.

> [This imperative] carries the tacit assumption that it is clear what needs to be done, that some impersonal guidance system like 'the market' or 'history' will determine what to do.

From the way that some Irish universities were reformed in the noughties, it was clear that their administrations were indeed in a great hurry to 'move ahead' and that some 'impersonal tele-guidance system' was indeed believed to be in place. Engell and Dangerfield distinguish between the wisdom of considered, balanced, proactive foresight on the one hand, and headlong hurry on the other.

> Reactivity – reflexive adaptation to every new thing – is not wisdom but hysteria. It can create a sense that immediate needs are the only ones worthwhile.

CAMPUS BUSINESS IV: GLOBAL BUBBLE-BLOWING

In Section Two of this book we saw that competition is at the heart of corporate rationale. In Higher Education the competitive imperative stretches to include competitive recruitment of staff and students. As already indicated, in Irish Higher Education, the pre-recession staff recruitment drive seems to have been centred on locally rather than internationally competitive hiring, with charges of staff 'poaching' being widely reported by the media. Certainly, the hiring fiesta of the mid- to late-noughties seemed to involve in practice, in some institutions at least, and especially for 'trophy' administrative positions, a surprisingly high proportion of national, inter-institutional or even intra-institutional appointments which came nonetheless at the cost of significant promotional and/or remunerative inducement. As such it could scarcely be regarded within the overall Irish Higher Education gene-pool as anything other than a costly game of musical chairs.

As for student recruitment, Irish universities often refer to the competition from top universities elsewhere who can recruit 'the best' students internationally with tempting scholarships. While this may be true of postgraduate students, for undergraduates it remains that, in terms of local student recruitment, Irish universities and colleges are remarkable for the very competitive tuition fees that they charge relative to what these students would be charged in the UK or the US. Given the current tight squeeze on exchequer funding, however, and even if the fees charged to domestic undergraduates are increased, funding will remain the single biggest challenge facing Higher Education (in Ireland as elsewhere). As we have seen, the worldwide trend is to address that challenge via commercial entanglements which, even if entered into with the best of intentions, either come with worrying strings, or raise uncomfortable questions. Before giving three Irish examples of such entanglements, it might be helpful to make one important observation. All three can and will be viewed either as 'good news' or as 'bad news' stories depending on what and whom we think Higher Education is for and depending on whether we think that the prices/costs of Higher Education are spiralling because of the system's flaws or because of its virtues and its ever-increasing worth.

Whither the Academic Independence of Irish Higher Educational Exports/Imports?

Example 1

An *Irish Times* headline on Tuesday, 28 September 2010 read as follows: 'China will co-finance new institute building at UCD, says Taoiseach.' The report, by Mary Minihan, outlined that Mr Cowen had met Li Changchun, the most senior Chinese politician to visit Ireland since prime minister Wen Jiabao in 2004. It further announced that the Irish Government was to co-finance with the Chinese authorities the development of a new, flagship building for the Confucius Institute at University College Dublin. According to the Government press office, 'this will be the first Confucius Institute internationally to receive capital funding from the Chinese authorities and testifies to the strong performance of the institute since it was established in 2006'. As the *Irish Times* report shows, the then Taoiseach's focus was on selling Ireland's brand: 'Mr Li made clear to me that Ireland's brand and reputation are very strong in China.' The article concluded, however, with a comment from the Executive Director of Amnesty International Ireland.

> Colm O'Gorman said it was important that trading relations with China were maintained and built on, but also criticised the Chinese administration: 'It's important that we build and maintain trading relations with a country like China. But this is also a government that detains thousands of men and women in prison or under house arrest simply because of their support for human rights,' Mr O'Gorman said. 'China is also the world's number one executioner. It is crucial that the Government makes clear in its contacts with the Chinese government the concerns of many Irish people about China's appalling human rights record.'

Eighteen months later, a different Irish government upscaled the Irish pitch to another Chinese government delegation, this time led by the Chinese Vice-President. In between the two most recent Chinese visits at least one of Ireland's major universities had signed a number of memoranda of understanding (on shared programmes and a joint campus) with various universities in China. On this most recent occasion, however, little or no room was made in the media or elsewhere for voices like those of the Amnesty director until the curtains had come safely down on the sales pitch of Ireland Inc.

Like their counterparts all over the world, Irish universities, as well as for-profit education companies such as Hibernia College, are very active in promoting links with Chinese universities. A fairly typical example would be the announcement in August 2011 of UCD's 'major medicine and biotechnology initiative in the heart of China's "Silicon Valley"'. This particular initiative involves a shared campus in China, a shared academic programme for Irish and Chinese students, and a post-graduate programme in translational medicine, that is, patient-driven drug development. Another UCD initiative is the establishment of a whole new International University as the second phase of a two-phase cooperation agreement with the Technological University of Beijing. It is, in fact, difficult to keep up with the pace of Sino-Irish twinning or collaboration initiatives within any single institution of scale.

What is worth considering in a little more detail here, however, is the status of what could be regarded as Ireland's seminal academic engagement with the Chinese government, namely UCD's Confucius Institute. The Institute dates from 2006 and has been extraordinarily successful from the Chinese perspective. So much so that it was twice, in rapid succession, awarded the distinction of being the Confucius Institute of the Year (in 2008 and 2010). Like Confucius Institutes elsewhere, it has also been very helpful to UCD, opening the door to a great number of bilateral Higher Education business links. UCC also has a Confucius Institute, and sub-institutes, called Confucius classrooms, have been established in other institutions, in NUI Maynooth, for example.

Hanban, the wing of the Chinese government concerned directly with the dissemination of the Chinese language and culture, controls China's Confucius Institutes abroad. There are currently about 500 Institutes all round the world and it is predicted that there will be 1,000 by 2020 in over 100 countries. They are mostly sited on university or college campuses and are often accompanied by 'Confucius classrooms' or outreach, aimed at disseminating Chinese not just at third-level but also at second level, providing, contracting – and usually paying – the Chinese teachers.

Ever since cultural institutes were first established as vehicles of so-called 'soft power' or cultural influence (Alliance Française, Cervantes Institutes, Goethe Institutes, British Council, and so on), they were located not on the campus of this or that university, but rather in cities. The delicate matter of intellectual independence is what makes all the difference between establishing a cultural institute controlled by another sovereign state anywhere else in a given country, rather than on a university or school campus. Although there has always been fruitful cooperation between the Goethe Institute and the Alliance Française and the departments of German and French of various Irish universities, these cultural institutes are entirely independent of universities and vice versa.

Some universities are on public record as being unwilling to host on-campus Confucius Institutes. For example, the University of Manitoba in Canada debated the matter exhaustively before deciding against authorisation. Because of the difficulty of proving a negative, it is impossible to know how many other universities worldwide were reluctant to sign up. As we have already seen, though, when the CORES academics of the University of Chicago signed a petition objecting to their University's choice of donors and sponsors, they challenged the University's by-passing of shared governance mechanisms in making those choices. It is perhaps worth noting again their specific concerns about the manner in which a Confucius Institute came to be sited on campus at the University of Chicago.

> Without consent of the faculty Senate, who are statuto-
> rily charged with exclusive jurisdiction in such matters,

University administration accepted the establishment of a Confucius Institute, an academically and politically ambiguous initiative sponsored by the government of the People's Republic of China. Proceeding without due care to ensure the Institute's academic integrity, it has risked having the University's reputation legitimate the spread of such Confucius Institutes in this country and beyond.

None of the US Ivy League universities appear to have invited Confucius Institutes on campus either, and *Yale Global online*, the official online publication of Yale University's Centre for the Study of Globalisation, enlarges as follows on the issues of propaganda and censorship that are particularly sensitive for universities as institutions which are, after all, subject to certain legal obligations to respect academic freedom.

Since 2001, China has funded nonprofit Chinese language institutes in nearly 100 countries. The institutes have since branched out into business and other areas while also funding scholarships and study in China. In an article for the *Asia Sentinel*, Glenn Anthony May of the University of Oregon points out that the centres of study come with conditions, including support for a one-China policy that denies recognition of Taiwan as a state. Donors influence campus management and presentations, and schools with Confucius Institutes may avoid open discussions on Tibet or the 1989 Tiananmen protest against Chinese government policies. He argues: 'Once the perks from Hanban begin to arrive, professors at universities with CIs become extremely reluctant to do anything to upset their generous benefactors.' Colleges have become complicit in Chinese propaganda and censorship, and May blames the Chinese scholars who comply with restrictions, yet understand the issues of history and need for free debate better than most.

May's *Asia Sentinel* article referred to by *Yale Global* is dated 4 March 2011 and is entitled 'China buys a sympathetic view in academe'. Another article by Don Starr published in the *European Journal of Education* (no. 44, 2009) refers to the exact nature of the concerns raised by some academics regarding on-campus Confucius Institutes. Apart from the human rights concerns raised by Amnesty's Colm O'Gorman in *The Irish Times* article quoted above, other issues mentioned in Don Starr's article (entitled 'Chinese Language Education in Europe: The Confucius Institutes') include: sustainability of financing from China and the availability from the host institutions of matching, long-term financial support; the academic viability of the institutes; the academic independence of any subsequent relations that might be brokered by Confucius Institutes with Chinese partner universities; the risk of facilitating political surveillance of the Chinese abroad; and finally, improper influence on academic matters in the host institution. The more specific issues on which censorship and propaganda fears are primarily focused include the treatment of those who fall foul of the political regime, including Falun Gong members. Indeed, coincidentally (given the bio-medical tenor of many of Irish Higher Education's academic links with its Chinese partners), Simon Coveney of Fine Gael was one of a number of (then) MEPs to call in 2006 for a full investigation into persistent rumours of Chinese human rights violations in relation to organ harvesting, specifically from Falun Gong detainees.

All of the 'educational independence' concerns mentioned above seem to have cristallised more clearly in countries physically closer to China. India has clear concerns in this respect. In the face of Chinese efforts to copperfasten its relay of navy bases in the Indian Ocean, India is particularly anxious to maintain a sort of *cordon sanitaire* around the Maldives archipelago. The prospect of a Confucius Institute in the Maldives (which have a population of just over 300,000) is not welcomed by India.

Similarly, Japanese public universities have long been resisting incentives to host the institutes. And as for Australia, an article published in the *Sydney Morning Herald* on 13 July 2011 reports the submission of a petition with 4,000 signatures to the parliament of New South Wales calling on the government to remove the 'Confucius Classroom' programme from a number of Sydney schools. The petition states that:

> The teaching of Chinese language and culture is welcome in NSW schools, but it should be available free from the influence of Chinese Communist Party doctrine and censorship.

According to the article:

> The sudden proliferation of institutes worldwide has prompted concerns that the Communist government is using the non-profit public centres as a tool to enhance its image. . . . Greens NSW MP John Kaye said impressionable students were being exposed to a 'biased view of Chinese history, human rights and world affairs . . .'

Only time will tell the truth about the ethical and economic cost/benefit equation regarding the question of who is in charge of, and who pays for, the teaching of Chinese at third (and second) level in Ireland. Two significant questions do arise in the immediate term, however. How is it that the issue of academic independence is crucial in some contexts, but not in others? And who decides when it needs to be debated, and when it can be brushed aside? And what does the 'brushing aside' do to the real and felt independence of Ireland's public colleges and universities?

Example 2

A further example of the stakes involved in Ireland's internationalisation of its Higher Education system concerns Malaysia. According to some local sources, Malaysia is fast becoming supersaturated with private medical schools. One of Ireland's universities has recently opened a new medical school in Malaysia, and two Irish colleges have been co-running another there for many years. There have been local expressions of concern not so much over the public/private tension or over the tuition fees at Malaysia's private medical schools, as over the availability of appropriate facilities for the provision of proper clinical supervision and experience for the hordes of students and interns issuing from all the institutions.

The situation appears to be as follows: with a population of about 28 million, Malaysia currently has approximately 30 medical schools, the vast majority of which are private. Up to 20 of these have sprung up in the last ten years. Most of these private schools are sponsored by foreign universities, public and private, based in the US, the UK, Australia and India for example, although some have been established by private (and foreign) healthcare interests other than universities. It appears, from a comparative survey of fees at 18 private schools, that the co-owned Irish school in Penang is one of the most expensive by some distance. However, the fact that a second Irish college is opening in a different province of Malaysia suggests that there is no shortage of demand for such an exclusive product. Apparently, the Malaysian public health system is experiencing a severe shortage of doctors because, curiously enough, qualified Malaysian doctors prefer to work in the more lucrative private sector. It is unlikely that the mushrooming of private schools will solve this problem, of course, since graduates are going to need to pay back the considerable debts that they will probably have incurred for their training. According to their website, the two Irish colleges net an annual fee income of 20 million euro through their joint Malaysian operation. To feel really dizzy, though, we have to look at the figures facing the student/client, which appear to be up to 15 times higher than those charged to domestic students.

It is important to note that the figures given here are neither official nor current. They were sourced in an online publication in 2005 of a comparative study of the costs of private medical studies in Malaysia. In fact, the website of the Irish medical college in Penang nowhere indicates the tuition fees that it charges. The only reference to tuition fees is an indirect rubric giving information on the arrangements made for 'study loans'. The fees quoted here in euros were valid for 2005 and may have risen in line with tuition fees in general. It should be said that a high proportion of the college's students are understood to benefit from federal and state financial support (scholarships) from Malaysia.

The real stroke of commercial genius for Irish Higher Education is that students enrolling in the Malaysian college spend the first two and a half or three and a half non-clinical years in Dublin. And the tuition fees charged for these Dublin years, which involve more of the less expensive 'bench' as opposed to 'bedside' tuition, are understood to be in excess of €30,000 per year. Moreover, while the clinical training of Ireland's Penang students, that is, their bedside apprenticeship, takes place almost entirely in Malaysia, the Irish economy benefits from their spending power over the approximately three years of their training in Dublin.

It is impossible for a layperson and outsider to weigh up the relevance of concerns expressed locally about the challenge associated (not just in Penang province but federally) with provision of appropriate levels, opportunities and intensity of clinical teaching, experience and supervision, given the pressure on the local teaching hospitals from all the medical schools operating in the country. It is also impossible to gauge from the outside how the future of such Irish investments is going to play out. In terms of the host temperature, though, it is interesting to note that, in contrast to at least one of its Irish contractors, Malaysia's largest national university, Universiti Sains Malaysia, makes no reference to 'global' ambitions nor to 'growth' in its promotional strap-line, which reads instead 'Transforming our universities for a sustainable future'. Moreover, in the summer of 2011 the university hosted a conference on the telling topic of the 'de-colonisation of Higher Education in South-East Asia'.

While being quite upfront about the principal purpose of this internationalisation exercise from the Irish perspective, name-ly raising the Irish colleges' non-exchequer funding, the Irish partners are understandably eager to highlight the mutually enriching cultural exchange associated with the Malaysian con-nection. Meanwhile, their Malaysian college's publicity material highlights that it is a 'not for profit' venture; in other words, it doesn't have private owners who can sell their shares or benefit personally in any taxable way. There can be absolutely no doubt, however, that this is a commercial and business operation first and foremost and through and through. Indeed, the extent and nature of the business orientation are striking. In 2011, certain information about the college was readily available online, but it is possible that this is no longer valid. The School does, however, appear to be still co-owned by the two Irish colleges and the Pen-ang State Industrial Development Corporation. Up to the sum-mer of 2011, the Dean of the college was also the chairman of the Joint Penang Independent Ethics Committee (JPEC). This com-mittee operates or operated, however, under the joint auspices of the Irish-run college medical school in Penang and a company called Gleneagles CRC, which makes it difficult to understand in what sense it can be said to be 'independent' or at least what exactly it is independent of. Gleneagles CRC, which also owns a medical school and clinical research centre in Penang province, seems to be owned by Parkway Healthcare, a company listed in Singapore and regarded as the largest private healthcare pro-vider in South East Asia. All details concerning the Joint Penang Independent Ethics Committee were sourced in 2011 on the web-site of a private company called Info Kinetics, a sort of one-stop clinical research operation centred on drug trials. The relation between the ethics committee (JPEC) and Info-Kinetics is explained on the latter's website as follows: 'JPEC conducts initial and continuing ethical review of clinical trials conducted in [the Irish-run college] under the coordination of Info Kinetics.' With a tag-line that reads 'connecting research and people', Info Kinetics was, according to its 2011 website, 'set up primarily to serve pharmaceutical companies in planning and conducting pharmacokinetic and clinical trials as well as to provide independent analytical services as part of their drug programme'. Certainly, a clear factor of the attractiveness of Info Kinetics for its pharmaceutical clients is its association with a private medical college, the Dean of which has been chairing the Joint Penang Independent Ethics Committee. A further bonus is the fact that, since the college is also part-owned by the Penang Industrial Development Corporation and because Info Kinetics is recognised as an R&D company by the Malaysian (federal) Industrial Development Authority, its client organisations, as the website puts it, 'enjoy a double tax exemption on the amount spent in Malaysia'.

Example 3

The Bahraini kingdom's 2011 crackdown on political and academic opposition to its authoritarian Sunnite regime put the National University of Ireland, more specifically one of its constituent colleges, into an impossible moral and financial position, embedded as it is to the tune of €60-70 million in brand new Bahraini bricks and mortar.

The Irish college's predicament was not entirely unpredictable, however. After all, the US- and Saudi-backed hardliner Prime Minister Khalifa Bin Salman Al Khalifa is the longest-ruling unelected Prime Minister in the world whose greatest ally was fellow-autocrat Saddam Hussein, at least until the latter invaded Kuwait. The Prime Minister had already flexed his muscles in 1997. Since then, he has consistently, in what looks like a classic 'bad cop, good cop' routine, appeared to undermine his apparently more progressive or moderate nephew, the current king, Hamad bin Isa al-Khalifa, who was awarded an honorary fellowship by the NUI college in 2006. This honour was followed in 2010 by an honorary Doctorate in Science for the Minister for Defence, also from the Al Khalifa clan. The regime's 2011 Saudi-reinforced crackdown on largely Shiite pro-democracy protesters put the US navy, which is based in Bahrain, under strong pressure from human rights organisations and political analysts alike to pull out of Bahrain and move to somewhere more stable like Oman. Unlike the mobile fifth fleet, however, the fine Irish-owned medical campus is, of course, stuck in the kingdom. Indeed, in a cruelly surreal twist of fate, the college's expensive Bahraini home is located in a city called Manama . . .

There was strong and timely international condemnation of a litany of human rights abuses committed by the Al Khalifa regime throughout the Arab Spring, from unlawful killings, imprisonments and torture to sham military trials and other denials of human and civil rights (the right of assembly, for example). Crucially, some of these abuses involved the victimisation of medics, academics and students, and some of the medics or medical academics were Irish-trained. These were accused by the regime not so much of treating its enemy as of refusing to treat or mistreating regime casualties and were accordingly targeted. Organisations protesting against that targeting included Amnesty International, Human Rights Watch and the UN Commissioner for Human Rights, as well as Physicians for Human Rights, Médecins sans frontières, the American College of Physicians, England's Royal College of Surgeons, the National Arab American Medical Association and the American Medical Association, and indeed several individual Irish medics and the Irish Nurses and Midwives Organisation. The public response of the Irish mother-college, however, was both tardy and lame, its hand-washing reflecting its highly compromised position of political, moral and financial subordination. The response of the Royal College of Physicians of Ireland was also compromising. In a letter published in *The Irish Times* in June 2011 the organisation implausibly refers to the forensic difficulty of deciding between the relative value of two conflicting views of what had 'really' happened in Bahrain: the Al-Khalifa view and the view of the victims as supported by all the organisations enumerated above. In other words, it claimed to believe that Bahrain's interrogation protocols and military courts would succeed in establishing the truth where its own delegation had failed: 'it is essential that the judicial process now underway is unequivocally fair and just, and clearly seen to arrive at the truth of what happened' (*The Irish Times*, 25 June 2011). As predicted by the human rights organisations, the 'judicial process' did no such thing and it was left to an independent investigation to confirm the full extent of the abuses. Meanwhile, the reputation of Irish Higher Education was further tarnished when it emerged that not only had the Irish college sung dumb in public after the dismissal of a sizeable number of Bahraini academics in the early days of the Spring of 2011, but it had obediently required some of its personnel and/ or students to sign what amounted to an oath of allegiance to the Al Khalifa regime. Between June 2011 and July 2012 neither those holding on to political power in Bahrain nor those protecting their investments there have changed their tune in any substantive way. Significantly, however, the National University of Ireland, of which the Bahraini college's parent institution is a constituent college, did eventually register its interest in the matter.

The above examples all suggest not only that the devil of internationalisation is in the detail, but also that the internationalisation of Higher Education and research (particularly in the biomedical field, presumably because of its income-generating powers), has a propensity – a paradoxical propensity in the case of biomedicine given the inherent nobility of the medical calling – to propel Higher Education into zones of particular ethical turbulence. It is interesting, for example, that drug development, or 'translational medicine' as it is also called, appears to be a particularly intense area of Irish academic trade and exchange with China. However, there is surely one significant difference between a venture like the newly inaugurated UCD-Shenzhen Institute of Health Science and Innovation, on the one hand, and the engagement signed in early 2012 between Ireland's principal for-profit college, Hibernia, and the extremely highly-ranked University of Peking. It might be reasonably expected that large-scale public universities incorporating colleges of arts and schools of philosophy will have thoroughly debated the ins and outs of all partnerships and sponsorships engaging the overall standing and standards of the university. But if this is so, then it's not happening out loud or in an open forum. Indeed, most academics working in Ireland's most globally invested not-for-profit universities would probably be hard-pressed to keep track of the mushrooming overseas joint ventures, in computer science or drug development alone for example, in which their universities are participating. Coinciding as they usually do with the heaping of honours such as honorary degrees, medals and distinctions upon the presidents of the universities in question and upon the representatives of the political regimes involved in the new collaborative ventures, these developments exert enormous silent traction on the ecosystems of Irish Higher Education. When some Irish university leaders boast about their institution's global formatting and footprinting, the implication is that the imperatives of Irish Higher Education and of the Irish state more generally are well served by such endeavours. If the opposite were the case, who is going to say so? And to whom? And who would listen?

Campus Business V: Corporate Consent and Academic Responsibility in Irish Higher Education

It will be obvious from much of the foregoing that one of the major casualties of the corporate university, Irish style, was transparent, deliberative and independent academic governance. While it is often argued that parliamentary-style debate and discussion is inefficient, it does provide for a modicum of checks and balances, and a semblance of democratic process. Instead of being elected by staff, the leaders of many if not most Irish universities are now selected by search and appointment committees. This is in keeping with a model in which presidents operate as CEOs at the apex of a top-down administration model which concentrates decision-making in executive committees which are to some extent hand-picked. In many cases, the result is, in part at least, a demoralised academic body which eventually comes to see itself as an ensemble of somewhat disenfranchised cogs turning busily in a giant machine run by transmission belt from a command centre that is in most meaningful respects, and at the very best *unreachable*. Of all the problems thrown up by this model, the most obvious is the cognitive dissonance between, on the one hand, the academic vocation, which involves the nurture of independent, critical and creative thinking, and on the other hand, an administration model based on centralised decision-making by a defensive legislature, executive and judiciary all rolled into one. In the most extreme Irish experiments with Apparat-run Higher Education institutions, the casualties have been the institution's credibility and even its legitimacy. And as one authority on managerialist culture astutely notes, (Rakesh Khurana, *From Higher Aims to Hired Hands*):

> Legitimacy is the currency of institutions . . . like trust, legitimacy can vanish very quickly, and, once lost, is difficult to regain. When an institution loses legitimacy . . . even everyday activities [are called] into question and perfectly sincere actions may be interpreted as [hiding] a hidden agenda.

Any loss of perceived legitimacy is obviously a particular problem for a public Higher Education institution. Arguably, though, this matter pales into insignificance in comparison with the national problem that arises for any small country when a significant section of its university system has allowed critical thinking to be so neutered that such obvious issues as the ones raised in this book are so seldom directly and openly addressed.

Quality: Hot and Cold Running PR

In belated post-Thatcherist mode, Irish Higher Education has been, for some time now, ratcheting up its quality assurance processes. Not only are all university and college units subject to regular quality review, but there are also regular 'whole institution' quality reviews. As far as can be seen with the naked eye, most of these exercises are benign. Moreover, in so far as they involve a degree of critical self-reflection and even some scrupulous external, peer-standard scrutiny, they may in some cases amply justify the resources that they devour.

If, however, Higher Education in Ireland is genuinely beset by the kinds of problems and dysfunction pointed up in this book, wouldn't we expect at least some of these issues to surface, however politely and euphemistically, in the ocean of quality review reports published online for all the world to read? If this is not the case, then what is the truth value of the reports generated in Irish academia by this pervasive 'quality' culture? And if so many real problems are not being named and identified in 'quality reviews', then what is the true purpose of such exercises?

Clearly, if they are to be worth the time spent reading them, let alone producing them, reviews of any kind must be properly focussed. If, therefore, the real and serious educational and academic issues described in this book are not finding expression in the flood of 'quality assurance' documentation generated by the corporate university, it might be because the quality system is not looking at the big picture of academic standards and educational integrity. If so, then what is the quality review system focusing on? And why?

If the body reviewing a given academic unit is not independent (if it is largely comprised of institutional insiders, for example), or if there is not a preponderance of competence in the specific academic area being reviewed, this deficit may also indicate that the review body is designed to measure something else, such as the unit's compliance with certain organisational goals, administrative structures or management processes, for example. Now it is manifestly clear that any inability or failure to audit what is supposed to be audited or any conflict of interest limiting the auditor's independence makes a complete nonsense of the entire exercise. Morevoer, in the audits conducted by Arthur Andersen of several businesses such as Enron, this very problem eventually wiped out not just Enron but a significant part of Arthur Andersen too.

It is interesting to consider one Irish university's recent 'whole institution' quality review in the light of this cautionary example. The review in question issued a broadly glowing report. Nonetheless, the latter included a telling recommendation. In all future internal quality reviews of individual cost centres, the reviewers recommended that the number of internal reviewers (from inside the institution) should not exceed the number of external reviewers, and that the reviews should not be chaired by employees belonging to the institution under scrutiny. Curiously, the report did not explicitly recommend that the purpose of reviews of academic, as opposed to administrative, cost centres is to assess the academic quality of the unit, rather than its compliance with commercial or managerial targets or goals. Nor that, in order to fulfil this role, the number of non-peer reviewers (from outside the discipline in question) should not exceed the number of peer reviewers (from inside the discipline). Perhaps the reason for these omissions is that in many corporate universities, academic 'cost centres' house several different disciplines, with the result that quality reviews cannot reasonably have peer reviewers on board for every single discipline represented, and so a properly 'academic' review of these mosaic units is a logistical and rational impossibility. Instead, a review of structural compliance has to be 'dressed up' to look like a review of academic quality.

The problem with disguises or charades of this nature is not that the websites of certain universities or colleges may be misleading their investors and clients in proudly displaying choice excerpts from reviews which have nothing at all to do with real academic quality, and which therefore bear little identifiable relation to the realities of Higher Education. Given that preening self-endorsement is standard issue in today's consumer culture, it is most unlikely that anybody is going to pay much attention to it, or that it will give any organisation an unfair competitive advantage on the national, international or global market. The problem is not, either, the waste of time: no sooner is one round of review over than another begins, all faithfully shadowing the hollow hyperbole of institutional mission statements, strategic plans, output targets and so on. The real difficulty is rather that any tolerance for bogus or fake assessment of academic value will inevitably further tighten the tissue of lies strangling the legitimacy and credibility of Higher Education from within. A recent *Times Higher Education* article (October 2011) by Anthony Oswald, professor of economics at the University of Warwick, comments on the critical importance of honesty in this respect.

> Corporations, pressure groups, government departments, churches, professional associations, trade unions and the rest all play a fundamental role in society; but none sticks up disinterestedly for the truth, because all have axes, whether small or large (and whether they acknowledge those axes or not), to burnish. They know what answers their organisations will tolerate. By contrast, [universities do] not. That is why dictators sometimes close them and why university quality assessments, if they measure real quality, can be a bulwark for society.

Irish Higher Education Policy: Where now?

In the Irish context, because the state is still the major source of Higher Education funding, the Irish government is a critical influence on the policies supported or jettisoned within the sector. Seen in that light, a speech made to the Royal Irish Academy by Ireland's Minister for Education on 30 May 2011 is most significant, largely because of its stereophonic quality. In other words, because of the way it speaks two languages.

On the one hand, the Minister's script demonstrates a real feel for the timeless truth of the educational relationship:

> The teaching environment in higher education should facilitate free discourse between student and teacher, stimulating the student to think critically, engage in higher order analysis, and learn to communicate and accommodate the views of others with tolerance.

Moreover, the speech explicitly underlines the importance of academic freedom for the functioning of a 'democratic republic' and for educating graduates able to think independently, in other words to be the kind of people that Irish 'society needs now more than ever if we are to grow and prosper with a new-found sense of pride and social justice'.

On the other hand, the RIA speech welcomes 'the priority given [in Higher Education to] improving the Quality of the Student Experience.' It especially supports 'the focus on providing a better first-year experience with . . . more opportunities to study across disciplines'. In a similar vein, the role of teaching feedback is highlighted:

> It is important that our students find their voice, engage fully in their own learning and clearly articulate their needs and opinion. An important element of this will be a full engagement of students with the development of feedback mechanisms at institutional and national level as they are implemented.

Further on, speaking the same language, the Minister states:

> If we are to deliver on our objectives for quality and responsiveness, there are certain system features that will need to be addressed as upfront implementation priorities. . . . we must deliver on the reforms committed to under Croke Park, including contract reviews, as an important starting point.

Similarly, he notes that 'the development of workload allocation models, and wider Croke Park reforms, will provide important building blocks'.

Some key sections of this speech suggest that Ireland's Minister of Education genuinely wants Irish Higher to facilitate critically engaged, articulate and tolerant citizenship within a socially just, democratic republic. However, breaking through that explicit commitment there is an alien discourse, the voice of an automaton. This voice talks the talk of 'quality assurance', 'performance accountability', 'reform', 'contract review', 'workload allocation models', 'feedback mechanisms', 'system features' and 'implementation priorities'. As we have seen, this is a globally replicant language and it is intimately linked to the distrust that has so thoroughly undone certain quarters of Higher Education in recent years. As such it is incompatible with the humane language of social justice and critically engaged citizenship. The problem is not that the two languages are on a collision course. It is, rather, that the collision has already taken place. And now the question is what can be salvaged from the crash, and how.

Public Service or Corporate Servitude? Academic Responsibility after Croke Park

As far as Higher Education is concerned, the academic reforms emerging from the Public Service Agreement signed at Croke Park, and informing the Minister's code-switching speech of May 2011, bear the clear imprint of the two bodies most often quoted in the Irish media in relation to Higher Education policy: namely, the Irish Universities Association and the Higher Education Authority. The IUA has a particularly interesting history. It began life as the CHIU or the Conference of Heads of Irish Universities. In the fullness of time, however, more precisely at the apogee of the Irish boom, this standing body (formally incorporated in 1997) grew itself a proper corporate structure. In 2005, it became the 'Irish University Association'. The seven directors are the seven Irish university presidents and the company lists not just a number of standing groups, such as the group of University Heads of Research, the group of University Registrars, and so on, but also a CEO who heads up a staff of a dozen or so executives (with responsibility for PR/Communications, International Relations etc.). The IUA's premises are on Merrion Square, next door to the National University of Ireland. The company is a member of IBEC (the Irish Business and Employers Confederation) as befits a body that represents the universities principally, if not exclusively, as 'Businesses' and 'Employers'.

Perhaps the most significant point about the IUA is that it speaks from within the ever-widening gulf that seems to separate academic employers on the one hand, and those academic employees who still see themselves as academics first and foremost, on the other. In recent times especially, the IUA has been acting as a sort of ouija board through which Irish senior university management appears to speak (to the media and to government, for example) with one voice on behalf of the entire Higher Education sector. That voice is, of course, identifiable as the automaton tone breaking through the Education Minister's speech. In addition to the important fact that the IUA 'medium' does not appear to have direct radio contact with the spirits of the Institutes of Technology, its ability to represent much less defend the imperatives of Irish Higher Education is limited by at least one other far more basic shortcoming, namely, its fundamental misunderstanding of the concept of academic responsibility. This misconception was made particularly manifest by recent controversies over the so-called Croke Park implementation plans.

When the 'Public Service Agreement' implementation plans drawn up by the universities were vigorously criticised as threatening academic freedom at a public meeting of academics held in Dublin in January 2011, the IUA responded to that criticism by issuing a significant press release. The position adopted by the IUA in that statement is so indirect and incoherent that it would be difficult for an outsider to make sense of it. For anybody familiar with the terrain, however, the message is clear. To begin with, the company declares its absolute commitment to the principle of academic freedom. But, in a manoeuvre of telling overkill, it then proceeds to cast three remarkably creative aspersions on the relevance of the principle of academic tenure as it currently applies to Irish academic contracts. First, it claims that academic tenure has little or nothing to do with academic freedom. Second, it holds that the academic tenure clause in Irish academic contracts is legally redundant, and therefore meaningless or pointless as a protection of the permanency of academic posts. And thirdly, it suggests that Irish Higher Education would be better off to jettison all mention of tenure in academic contracts since the term 'tenure' is linked in the public mind to the notion that delinquent academics are undismissable.

On the face of it, to suggest that the principles of academic tenure and academic freedom are not indissociably linked is like claiming that there's no link between universal suffrage and democracy. The principle of academic tenure or security of academic employment is widely recognised as the chief guarantee of academic freedom. However threatened its current status, it has long been the lynchpin of US Higher Education. To quote Michael Roth (the President of Wesleyan University in the US) again:

> Tenure is surely an imperfect system, but I haven't found
> an alternative that provides sufficient protection of aca-
> demic freedom.

Regarding the point about the Irish public misconstruing academic tenure as shielding academic delinquency, it is so easily answered that it must be suspected of being a red herring. The fact is that, when it is properly respected by university management, academic tenure cannot constitute a shield for professional incompetence or misconduct. Thus, two North American studies, dated 1994 (in the *Higher Education Chronicle*) and 2005 (in the *Wall Street Journal*), estimate respectively at 50 and 50-75 the average number of senior tenured academics who had their tenure revoked 'for just cause' annually in the US.

Deliberately or not, the IUA's cautionary reference to the urban myth of unsackable rogue academics, and indeed its contorted dance around the issues of academic tenure and freedom, divert attention from three crucial matters. First, they are distractions from the far more likely cause of most of the negative publicity and even fury currently being directed at Irish academics and universities. For example, there was the repeated (televised) performances of some senior university managers in front of the Dáil's Public Accounts Committee, where they stoutly defended the allegedly unauthorised and unlawful performance bonuses awarded to senior academic managers over several years. Secondly, the elephant in the room in the IUA discussion of tenure is the spectre of natonal bankruptcy and of largescale involuntary redundancies. We have already seen that some US universities are coming close to this doomsday scenario. Thirdly, in focusing on 'rogue' academics, attention is diverted from the following two facts. One: picking out a couple of rotten apples will not save a system at risk of collapse under an excessive cost burden. Two: if administration posts outnumber academic posts in a ratio of three to two, and if payroll is the greatest Higher

Education cost, then the top-heavy, low-hanging fruit threatening to break the university branches are not necessarily, or not principally, academic.

Regardless, then, of what the IUA statement says or does not say about tenure or academic freedom, the signs are all pointing towards an Irish Higher Education system staffed by two separate tiers of academic employees: the first highly-salaried top tier will consist of a cadre of lead executives spread across government, quangos, think tanks etc., as well as the senior management of Higher Education institutions themselves and a mobile cadre of top (that is, income-generating) academic experts/consultants more at home in the Larry Summers than in the Derek Bok school of thought. The lower second tier will consist of a large army of disposable 'adjuncts' or piece-workers, just like in the US. As the robocop lingo of the revised academic contract clearly signals, this business dream is gradually being hardwired into Irish Higher Education. At its heart lies a profound betrayal of the concept of academic responsibility.

Internationally and historically speaking, what is important about academic tenure is not so much that it protects academic freedom by shielding principled academics from retaliatory or repressive measures up to and including termination. The really significant point about the tenure clause is that it defines and protects *not* so much academic freedom as the flip side of the same coin: academic responsibility. It stipulates that academics must answer not merely to their employer but to a whole set of academic values shared by the wider academic community. Thus at the University of Houston, one of the 'reasonable grounds' on which academics can have their tenure revoked include committing any action that 'would result in a general condemnation of the faculty member *by the US academic community*' [my italics]. Similarly, at the University of Rochester, tenure can be revoked should an academic fail 'to discharge responsibly his or her fundamental obligations as a teacher, colleague, and *member of the wider community of scholars*' [my italics]. As we saw in the first section of this book, the plan for Irish Higher Education is, apparently, to revise the academic contract in such a way as to refer the primary responsibilities of academics to the corporate person of the individual university as employer. This will surely have an impact on the intellectual independence of academics. For example, under those revised terms, this book could reasonably be seen as hostile to certain commercial and operational interests and aims of this author's employer and as such as a breach of contract.

Arthur O. Lovejoy and John Dewey founded the American Association of University Professors in 1915. Their '1915 Declaration of Principles on Academic Freedom and Academic Tenure' underlines the importance of distinguishing between the academic's responsibilities as an academic, on the one hand, and as a 'corporate' employee, on the other. In fact, for the authors of this declaration, academics had to be distinguished from 'ordinary employees' of academic institutions because:

> . . . in the essentials of [an academic's] professional activity [his or her] duty is to the wider public to which the institution itself is morally amenable.

The year 1940 saw the publication of a further landmark document on the question, the 'Statement of Principle on Academic Freedom and Tenure', which similarly articulates quite a taut relation between the public good on the one hand, and the interests of the employer institution on the other.

It is not, and never has been, easy to define either the nature of the academic's duty to the 'wider public' or even to define the 'wider public' in question. Two things are clear, however. One: the 'public' whom academics in Ireland are paid to serve is not limited to their employer's 'sponsors and clients'. It includes, rather, the whole social, political and educational ecosystem in which the university or college operates. Not just our own students, for example, but all the secondary school pupils who are taught by university-educated teachers. Two: if the strategic plan of Ireland's largest university is entitled 'forming global minds', then the public to which Irish Higher Education is 'morally amenable' is actually quite vast. It includes not just our overseas sponsors and clients, but also the entire eco-system to which those sponsors and clients belong. Indeed, Irish Higher Education is arguably 'morally amenable' to all whom our 'business plan' obliges us to ignore, exclude or even trample as we expand what one Irish university has taken to calling its 'global footprint'. Furthermore, if Irish Higher Education allows itself to be used as a laundering service for global financial forces that might be ultimately associated, via opaque and virtually untraceable flows, with interests ultimately destructive rather than protective of the intrinsic values of higher education or of values such as justice and equality of opportunity, then our Higher Education system has far wider planetary responsibilities than we might ever have imagined.

Maybe there is no need to fear that the proposed revision of Irish academic contracts will (further) pressure Higher Education towards targets aligned with the often questionable interests of global financial capital. And maybe, although they are currently dragooned into thinking there is no alternative, the less enlightened of Irish college handlers will join with the exceptionally enlightened few in refusing to squeeze Higher Education and its various ideals even further and harder down a deadly corporate rabbit-hole. But if not, then who or what will be left to oppose the rule of fakes and proxies, or to call time on the culture of branding and corporate control?

4

Higher Education for 'Living in Truth'

PRESCRIPTIONS?

The opening lines of a review of *A Manifesto for the Public University* (2011) underline the limitations of this book's account of 'academic Armageddon':

> After years of quiet preparation, the Blitzkrieg against the public university is unfolding across such a massive front that no one scholar can stake out an adequate line of defence.

So writes Howard Hotson, a professor of Intellectual History at Oxford.

Academic Armageddon makes no claim to objectivity. It is written from within scorched terrain. It is neither a commissioned report nor a scholarly study. Above all, it does not presume to prescribe a cure for the ills it names. A plethora of commissioned diagnoses and prescriptions, including the Hunt report – aka the 'National Higher Education Strategy'– can be consulted on the website of Ireland's Higher Education Authority. One of the more recent, issued in early October 2011, is a discussion document on a proposed 'National Academy for the Enhancement of Teaching and Learning'. Other recent proposals published by the HEA are entitled 'Towards a Future Higher Education Landscape'; 'Process and Criteria for Designation as a Technological University'; and 'Guidelines on Regional Clusters'. It might be expected that experienced frontline academics and educationalists would have had a major input into these proposals, but that does not always appear to have been the case. Far more worryingly, the fixer-bodies charged with setting Higher Education policy in Ireland do not appear to have derived much benefit from something that should, in theory, have positioned them very favourably in one vital respect: the availability of clear directions to cautionary academic graveyards – both in Ireland and beyond – where the academic standards upheld by once-flourishing departments and faculties fell foul of thoughtless 'restructuring' and/or 'clustering'; where 'quality enhancement' morphed into asphyxiating micro-management; and where participative academic governance, along with core academic values and standards, were taken over by a deadly kind of first-degree commercial instrumentalism that must have John Henry Newman writhing in his tomb.

Perhaps, though, before Irish Higher Education commissions or implements any new prescriptions, it should consider the extent to which it is already suffering from the effects of mis-prescription. Where commercialist or managerialist paradigms have been most aggressively applied by Higher Education systems, whether in the US, in the UK or in Ireland, have they propelled their adepts towards stellar standards of research and education? Whether in New Haven or Belfield, Gower Street or St Stephen's Green, or indeed off-shore (in Sri Lanka, Singapore, Malaysia, Dubai, China, Saudi Arabia, Bahrain) have they produced thinking that is demonstrably more critical, more creative or more independent? Have they produced graduates or post-graduates who think in greater depth, can see round more corners, anticipate more potholes or show a greater appreciation of complexity and greater mastery of detail? And if so, where – with respect – is the evidence?

Given that raw quantum or plumped-up proxies (more universities, more graduates, more PhDs, more publications, more patents, more credits, more As, bigger offices, fatter bonuses, higher tuition fees, more subordinates in the management line) have no probative value in this respect, there has to be some doubt about the answer to this question. What is absolutely certain, however, is that the business management paradigm has incurred malignant administration costs and prices wherever it has been applied. And it is also clear that these spiralling costs have sucked some institutions into a desperate vicious circle which involves essentially turning a blind eye to educational and academic issues in order to focus exclusively on growth and competition. And all too often this means turning Higher Education itself – often with the complicity of government if not at its express demand – into an export-led business.

There is no denying that some universities have sufficient genuine academic traction and sufficient budgetary upholstery to play that game with impunity. Harvard, Yale, Oxford, Cambridge and Princeton, for example, all have self-fulfilling, rock-solid academic reputations both domestically and worldwide. Arguably, only one Irish university has anything approaching equivalent 'academic name recognition'. As for endowment cushions, Yale's was worth $19.4 billion in the year ending June 2011. And although this represents an improvement on the crash situation in which $6.5 billion were wiped off its endowment value, Yale is still running a deficit, is actively cutting back on its running costs and has set up shop (as we saw earlier) in Singapore.

The problem facing Irish Higher Education on the global pitch is not so much the fact that even loans like 2011's €90 million loan for UCD from the European Investment Bank (which also loaned €450 million to universities in Spain) are only going to plug one small hole, allowing the completion of a few important capital investment projects. It is not so much that, like even some of the best-off of European universities, Irish Higher Education is sitting on cold, bare economic rock. It's rather that the current regime of cutbacks and stepped-up commercialism is – in some key cases – coming hot on the heels of an Irish boom-time orgy of pseudo-academic bling, as uncherished academic subjects had their assets stripped and reinvested (that is, sunk) in commercial tinsel. Unpalatable as it may be, the analogy that comes to mind here is the culinary one attributed to the Polish dissident President, Lech Walesa: it's easier to turn the tropical fish into chowder than to turn the fish soup back into an aquarium.

So is it going to be possible to find our way back (or forward, or sideways?) to a genuinely public-spirited academic gold standard? And if so, then how? If this book had the answer to that question it would also have the answer to the systemic ills besetting UK and US Higher Education. Moreover, it would presume to have the answer to the social democratic deficit that is currently undoing the public goods of so many states worldwide. As it is, the book's contribution is limited in the main to pointing up some of the dangers of a uniquely asphyxiating Higher Education fixation on US-led commercialism and UK-led managerialism.

IRELAND'S CALL?

In his 2011 book, from which I will quote again further on, New York University historian Tony Judt gives some insight into the contempt in which the strutting of Ireland Inc. was held by some external observers in boom times.

> Although uncritical admiration for the Anglo-Saxon model of 'free enterprise', 'the private sector', 'efficiency', 'profits' and 'growth' has been widespread in recent years, the model itself has only been applied in all its self-con-

gratulatory rigor in Ireland, the UK and the USA. Of Ireland there is little to say. The so-called 'economic miracle' of the 'plucky little Celtic tiger' consisted in an unregulated, low-tax regime which predictably attracted inward investment and hot money. . . . When Wall Street's party crashed, the Irish bubble burst along with it. It will not soon reflate.

These are hard words. But of course the Celtic Tiger could be, in its time, equally contemptuous of those whom it deemed to be out-and-out losers, like 'the French' who – ante-Sarkozy or anti-Sarkozy – still appeared to believe in large numbers in something reminiscent of 'social democracy'. Whatever about contempt, it would be difficult to overestimate the dismay with which political analysts from the oppositional European Left viewed what they regarded as the official death certificate of democracy in the European Union: namely, the subjection of the Irish population to a repeat referendum not just on the Nice Treaty but on the Lisbon one too. The title of one academic study on this topic, translated into French and published in France is 'Democracy for Sale'. Shortly after the event, the Left Front politician Jean-Luc Mélenchon also acidly observed the transformation of the 'Celtic Tiger' into a 'Cowering Kitten'. Later on, Mélenchon again gave the 'Celtic Tiger' image prominence in his 2012 presidential election campaign. Suggesting that Nicolas Sarkozy might have a better chance of being elected in Germany than re-elected in France, Mélenchon noted that neo-liberals always need a model: first, he said, it was the 'little Celtic Tiger', now it is Germany, a geriatric retirement age and the urgency of taking a job – *any* job, at *any* wage – to have any social entitlements.

So to what extent is the international reputation of Irish Higher Education doomed to follow that of the deluded Tiger economy? Is it not possible that Ireland is at some advantage when it comes to the various impasses discussed in this book?

First, there is the fact that the country has just woken up to its involvement in a large-scale scam in which our collective critical faculties were disabled. As a result, the entire Irish people, like the Greeks and the Icelanders, now know – viscerally – just how possible it is for a whole country or set of countries, to be taken in by a huge swindle.

Second, there is our historical and cultural familiarity both with loss and with looking outwards. Our experience as survivors of loss includes both permanent and temporary surrenders: of our own language, of our political independence, our emigrants, and most recently, of our prosperity, our economic self-confidence and sovereignty. As for our history of outward-looking engagement with the world, this ranges from monastic forays into Europe during the Dark Ages to the entrepreneurial Wild Geese; from our more cabin-feverish writers and artists to the coffin ships of the Great Famine; from Catholic missionaries to the UK building-site navvies; and today a new wave of outward economic exiles (balanced to some degree by what fortunately remains of boom-time inward migration). This historical experience of subordination and loss but also of outward-looking resilience gives Ireland a small advantage once we don't forget to stir in important grainy details. Such as the fact that the Church that sent our monks and missionaries, saints and scholars out to light up the Dark Ages is the same one that a millennium later not only fulfilled an essential duty of educational and nursing care offloaded onto it by an indeed green 'republic', but also gave shelter to the diabolical abuse of the defenceless. Or the fact that some of the most entrepreneurial of Ireland's Wild Geese were the most successful of Haiti's slave-traders and slave-owners with one family notably making its fortune in the triangular trade in human beings and sugar (setting up the infamous Angola company). Later on, some of the young state's choices would ensure that the history of Ireland's solidarity with the hunted and with the betrayed of Europe and the world is a mixed and ambivalent one. Yet that – sometimes shaming – history, when added to the sobering awakening from delusions of economic omnipotence, surely gives Ireland a head-start on understanding where Higher Education might be going wrong and/or failing humanity, and on imagining alternative routes?

Thus far, understandably, the Irish imagination engine seems to be flooded. Instead of serene, creative responses, Ireland's economic collapse has launched an almost hysterical frenzy of strategising in Higher Education. Reactive panic is perhaps an inevitable part of adjustment to any large-scale trauma. Disappointingly, however, one element has remained constant through both boom and bust, namely, the identification of (national and individual) economic gain as being the chief purpose of education. Moreover, the means of achieving this end are still widely held to be the increase of managerial and administrative control over the educational process. It is difficult to see anything substantively changing as long as this view drowns out all others. If the ethos of Higher Education is to change for the better, then it must find a way to respect values such as truthfulness and trustworthiness more than profit or prestige. It must value real democracy and real social and human solidarity. It must stop representing the world exclusively as a market and education as a product.

As a small, diversified society with a part to play within a particular continent, Ireland surely needs to be able to name very clearly what purpose we want our Higher Education system to serve and – unless we really believe that things are fine as they are and that we boast the best-educated population in the world – what exactly we would like to change about it. It just won't work any more to trade on our Anglo-nation currency or to continue marching blindly down the road behind our beleagured American or UK cousins. Nor will it suffice to bandy about words like 'access' or 'quality' or 'excellence', because they have no stable meaning of their own. The meaning of these words depends on what we are opening access to; what is being measured as 'excellent' or 'top quality' and what end it serves. The same goes for 'key performance indicators', an expression that begs the question as to what is being 'performed', for whom and for what? And as for the sinister expression 'fit for purpose', in the absence of any acceptable definition of the said purpose, it is far worse than meaningless. In a world where many institutions and individuals are utterly disoriented concerning the meaning and value of just about everything – work, family, life, culture, education, religion, money, nature, politics, language, art – this expression, more than any other, suggests an unconvincing and even frightening level of certainty about the 'purpose' for which the 'fitness' of people's education or work is to be adjudicated upon. It is no accident that a recent French-made film called *Heartbeat Detector* – perhaps one of the most chilling yet entirely inexplicit films ever made about the Shoah, focussing on the excellence and quality control of the Nazi genocide-management operation – is set in a large present-day business corporation. The film centres on the often-noted analogy between the de-humanised language of Darwinian corporate management (depersonalisation, rationalisation, streamlining, output maximisation, etc.) and the sanitised language used by the agents of the Holocaust's unsurpassed horror.

If we are serious about wanting Higher Education to foster deep, subtle, critical and creative thinking, if we want it to be even minimally open to the uncertainty and self-questioning that are surely the preconditions for imaginative and original thought, then we need to do something about the 'structures and processes' approach to Higher Education that prevails not just in some of our most damaged institutions but also above, beyond and around them. We're going to have to re-examine these and other approaches which take not just the maturity, humanity and dignity out of Higher Education, but also the critical depth, subtlety and imaginativeness without which it will atrophy: I'm thinking of the various approaches analysed throughout this book, such as the privatisation and casualisation of academic work; the concerted infantilisation of students as consumers of an 'experience'; the imposition of a uniform customer-controlled approach to course delivery; the primitive, Pavlovian commercialism of performance-related pay for income-generating academics and performance-related funding for strategically aligned research productivity.

As this book goes to press, colleagues in the Irish Colleges of Education, which educate primary-school teachers, appear to be having some difficulty fending off challenges to the status of what are termed 'academic' subjects such as history or English literature or French. This is surely reminiscent of the challenge issued by former French president Nicolas Sarkozy to the entrance examination for the ultra-prestigious École Nationale d'Administration which requires of candidates that they be able to discuss certain classic literary works. The example taken by Sarkozy was, unfortunately for him, one of the most exquisite, most delicately-written stories ever of the conflict between passion and duty, *La Princesse de Clèves*. Why on earth, the then President scoffed, would any senior French public servant, politician or business tsar/ina want or need to have to read this seventeenth-century yawn? This in a country where 500,000 secondary school pupils have opted to study Latin or Greek or both up to baccalaureate level. The chief discernible public response to this boo-boo (the vulgarity of which was never really lived down by the former President of a people who still pride themselves on their intellectual refinement and cultural sophistication) was a rocketing of sales of the classic. The fact is that most parents – world-wide – surely want the people who teach their children to be both pedagogically skilled and highly educated individuals. If primary school teachers emerge from college having authentically pursued an academic subject such as history, mathematics, French, music and so on to degree level, how can that be a problem? Conversely, surely anything that might undermine the student teacher's own educational development, academic interests or cultural enthusiasm is bound to depress the educational ethos not just of our our Colleges of Education but also of our primary schools.

Cast Out from the 'Feast of Life'

It is important to return here to the early 2011 statement of the current chairman of the Irish Higher Education Authority, a statement that in many ways prompted the writing of this book. The general idea was that the humanities need to explain what they are for, whereas the value of the scientific or technological disciplines, for example, is self-evident. For several millennia now, the value of the humanities has rested principally on the Socratic notion that the 'unreflected' or 'unexamined' life is not worth living. If, however, the point of the humanities is to help to ensure that, as universally as possible, human beings can live lives that are worth living, we would surely have to agree that this is the purpose of education in general, and not just of education in the humanities. Furthermore, any educator, any academic, in the sciences or in the humanities, is aware first of all of the narrowness of what they study or know and the vastness of all they don't study or know. This is why a searching uncertainty is the hallmark of any person, student or teacher, scientist, humanist, artist or seer who has glimpsed the infinitely receding horizon of complete understanding of even the smallest of questions.

Theodore Roszak, in the 1995 preface to his 1969 flower-power book *The Making of a Counter Culture*, wrote that 'education' has become 'a matter of machine-tooling the young to the needs of our various bureaucracies: corporate, governmental, military, trade union, educational'. He also recalled that, not long before he died, 'the greatest scientific mind since Newton' (Albert Einstein) confessed that if he had known what was going to be done with the fruits of his research in physics, namely the incineration of the citizens of Hiroshima, he would have become a shoemaker instead of a scientist.

> There is in the great man's lament a pathos too deep any longer to be appreciated by the sorcerer's apprentices who crowd forward in disconcerting numbers to book passage on the technocratic gravy train. And where the scientists and technicians lead, the pseudoscientists and social engineers are quick to follow. Given the dazzling temptations of a sky's the limit research circus, what time is there to dally over traditional wisdom or moral doubt? It distracts from the bright, hard, monomaniacal focus that pays off for the expert.

Roszak is referring here principally to the hard sciences, although he also mentions expertise in social 'engineering'. Surely, however, most contemporary academics – even in the arts and humanities – would recognise their own increasingly pressured and monomanical world of research and expertise in Roszak's comments. For the world in which most academics work today is indeed, as Roszak suggests, increasingly closed to all dalliance with the value of 'traditional wisdom'. That pressure can be countered, of course. And surely it must be countered and resisted insofar as it has the power, in the words of James Joyce (from the story 'A Difficult Case' in *Dubliners*), to turn us and our children into outcasts 'from the feast of life'.

If there was one change that could re-focus Higher Education on 'the feast of life' and on the fact that all humanity is in the same uncertain boat, what would it be? Surely it would be the restoration of respect for the full diversity and intrinsic value of all humane work, wisdom and skill. Perhaps we all do respect deep down the diverse and intrinsic value of all humane being and doing, including (but not above any or all) academic work. Yet the systems and structures organising our world militate against our ability to live by that respect.

OTHER TIMES, OTHER HOAXES

When the work of a thinker, a poet, a painter, a critic, a scientist, a writer, a dissident, a mathematician, a journalist, a historian, a politician puts a shape for us all on some timeless or original insight, that is the moment that most academics live for. The more brilliant minds create those moments for others; the less brilliant appreciate and amplify them. If this book is so full of the 'words of others' it is because it is, essentially, a bracelet of such insights into contemporary academia.

The Chinese writer Gao Zingjian is a case in point. This writer was forced to serve a 're-education' sentence during the Cultural Revolution. In the early 1980s, he accepted political asylum in Paris and was declared persona non grata in China after he criticised the Tiananmen Square massacre. In his Nobel Prize acceptance speech, entitled 'The Case for Literature' (2000), Gao Zingjian comments on freedom and markets.

> In the present age . . . the market economy has become pervasive and books have also become commodities. Everywhere there are huge undiscriminating markets. . . . If the writer does not bend to the pressures of the market and refuses to stoop to manufacturing cultural products by writing to satisfy the tastes of fashions and trends, he must make a living by some other means. Literature is not a best-selling book or a book on a ranked list and authors promoted on television are engaged in advertising rather than in writing. Freedom in writing is not conferred and cannot be purchased but comes from an inner need in the writer himself. . . . If one exchanges freedom for something else then the bird that is freedom will fly off.

Other writers or thinkers who have reflected on the really big questions of truth and freedom at the heart of the realities of academic Armageddon, are the great defector, Czeslaw Milosz, and the great dissident, Vaclav Havel.

THE CAPTIVE MIND

Historian Tony Judt's poor opinion of Ireland's boom-time choices has already been quoted here. Judt, who was Professor of History at New York University until his premature death in 2010 from motor neurone disease, wrote a lot towards the end of his life about intellectual freedom. He was an outspoken Jewish critic of the US Zionist lobby, a position that cannot have been easy to maintain. As such, Judt was a loyal friend to his fellow academic, the Palestinian cultural critic Edward Said, Professor of Literature at Columbia University until the latter's equally un-timely death from leukemia in 2003. As independent and con-trarian thinkers, Judt and Said both depended heavily on aca-demic and intellectual freedom in order to be able to live, write and work freely and in peace in the US. In a blog run by the *New York Review of Books* Judt wrote a very forthright article about hoaxes called 'Captive Minds, Then and Now'. In it he studies how the mindset of Soviet intellectuals forced to live with the Communist scam resonates with the situation of Western intel-lectuals today. The title of Judt's article refers to the writer Cze-slaw Milosz, who was brought up in Poland during the two world wars, surviving the Soviet occupation. Milosz was sent to Paris as cultural attaché for the new People's Republic of Poland but he defected to the West in 1951. His influential book, *The Captive Mind*, appeared two years later. As Judt notes:

> . . . never out of print, it is by far the most insightful and enduring account of the attraction of intellectuals to Stalinism and, more generally, of the appeal of authority and authoritarianism to the intelligentsia.

Tony Judt's account of Milosz's thinking makes fascinating reading for anybody interested in how ideological and institu-tional scams operate, and more especially for anybody who won-ders how and why otherwise intellectually acute minds manage to come to some sort of accommodation with the most delusional, totalitarian systems of groupthink. Explaining Milosz's reference to the Eastern notion of 'ketman', Judt continues:

> Those who have internalised the way of being called 'Ketman' can live with the contradictions of saying one thing and believing another, adapting freely to each new requirement of their rulers while believing that they have preserved somewhere within themselves the autonomy of a free thinker – or at any rate a thinker who has freely chosen to subordinate himself to the ideas and dictates of others.

What is most arresting about Tony Judt's reading of Milosz is the comparison he makes between 'captive minds' in Milosz's time and in ours. As Judt eloquently puts it:

> Our disability is discursive: we simply do not know how to talk about [the possibility of imagining alternatives to the choice between capitalism and communism] any more. For the last thirty years, when asking ourselves whether we support a policy, a proposal or an initiative, we have restricted ourselves to issues of profit and loss – economic questions in the narrowest sense. But this is not an instinctive human condition; it is an acquired taste.

This observation recalls the analysis of an Australian academic, Arran Gare, in an article tellingly entitled 'The Neo-Liberal Assault on Australian Universities and the Future of Democracy: The Philosophical Failure of a Nation'. Gare writes that 'it has become a major undertaking to show that the transformation of the education system is undermining democracy because people no longer understand the words needed to argue this.' Or, as the philosopher of globalisation, Ulrich Beck, aptly put it, distinctions between concepts such as 'democratic' and 'anti-democratic', freedom and un-freedom, are currently beyond our reach. As a result, the world is covered, according to Beck, in a deep layer of cognitive mould or 'verbal mildew'.

Surely today, now that it is caught in a feudal debt-trap, Ireland is gradually learning about how democracy can be undermined under our noses. But Gare is right. If educational 'value' only means value for money, then it is not surprising that we are barely able to see the distinction between real and fake democracies, let alone that this distinction matters. In other words, it is surely inevitable that a whole range of countries either openly ruled by dictatorship or democracies in name only will simply appear as open for business or not, as available or unavailable markets, for our (educational) product. Thus Cuba is still fairly closed, but China is wide open for business; Burma is closed, Singapore wide open; North Korea and Iran are closed, Bahrain and Dubai are open. Who could be surprised that some sections of Irish Higher Education, desperate to 'reflate' the burst bubble of its aims and ambitions, is particularly keen to trade on those open markets, whatever that avidity may say about respect for the principle of democracy. This political neutrality is not a new blight, either in Ireland or more generally. The eighteenth-century French educationalist, Marquis de Condorcet, commenting on the expansionist capitalism of his day, wrote with evident dismay that soon freedom will only exist 'in the eyes of an avid nation', as the 'necessary condition for the security of financial transactions'.

Tony Judt believed that the state of mental captivity described by Milosz is actually not so very far removed from the ideological imprisonment prevailing in our new millennium:

> . . . there is more than one kind of captivity. Recall the Ketman-like trance of those intellectuals swept up in George W. Bush's hysterical drive to war just a few years ago.

Judt then widens out this diagnosis of contemporary human captivity way beyond the delusions of state communism and way beyond the neo-con hoax of those who used lies to sell the Iraq war to the terrorised West. For him, 'the true mental captivity of our time lies [in our] contemporary faith in "the market"'. As Judt points out, like fascism or communism, the market 'has its true believers . . . its fellow travelers – who may privately doubt the claims of the dogma but see no alternative to preaching it; and its victims.' If the power of an ideology can be measured by a 'collective inability to imagine alternatives', then the power of unregulated markets and rampant consumerism (including cultural and educational consumerism) is close to being absolute in our age.

Such was the response to Tony Judt's *New York Times* article about the free market hoax that he used the last months of his life to expand it into a book that was published by Penguin in 2011. Apart from explicitly singling Ireland out for the blistering irony with which he refers to the 'plucky little Celtic Tiger', as we already saw, Judt's book gives the country further prominence by entitling the whole volume *Ill Fares the Land*. This title is borrowed from the book's epigraph, a quotation from the Irish writer Oliver Goldsmith, author of *The Deserted Village* (1770). The epigraph reads: 'Ill fares the land, to hastening ills a prey/ Where wealth accumulates, and men decay.'

Judt's book as a whole is fundamentally about the ravages of unrestrained market capitalism in the US and in Europe, although it also references the forgotten victims of globalisation, the tens of millions of slumdwellers in and around cities like Lagos or Lima. He identifies the demise of social democracy and the consequential explosion of (income) inequality as the double axis of market capitalism. Referring to the correlation of inequality with poverty, ill-health, mental illness and crime, and quoting Richard Wilkinson and Kate Pickett's book *The Spirit Level: Why More Equal Societies Almost Always Do Better*, he notes that the West is shell-shocked by the current economic crisis. Most significantly, in *The Memory Chalet*, Judt deplores the relentless lowering of academic standards as a would-be fix for an economic problem. He argues that, although it only produces a flattened, anti-academic uniformity, dumbing-down mendaciously masquerades as a solution to inequality (of opportunity).

RESISTING LIES

Without using the term 'ketman', Vaclav Havel, the writer and former Czech dissident/President, also wrote extensively, in his book *Living in Truth*, for example, about the implications of playing along with large-scale hoaxes. Havel was especially interested in the psychology of those who 'know better', but who still live lives that have been turned into a 'kind of endless dissimulation'. For him, the communist regime was only able to function because people were able to improve their status and sometimes even their material circumstances, however minimally, by obediently operating the giant scam:

> Think what you like in private, so long as you agree in public, refrain from making difficulties, suppress your interest in truth and silence your conscience – and the doors will be wide open to you.

Havel's description of the careerists and opportunists whom he labels 'typical collaborators' is unforgiving:

> If the principle of outward adaptation is made the keystone to success in society, what sort of human qualities will be encouraged and what sort of people, one may ask, will come to the fore?

But then, as a dug-in dissident, Havel had personally seen and felt the bared teeth of the totalitarian guard-dogs, whereas Milosz had avoided this experience by his early defection.

One of the most comforting aspects of Havel's approach to resistance is that he gives dissidents permission not to be able to imagine an alternative to the totalitarian system in place. This is helpful because the fact is that there would be no dissidents at all, ever, if to dare to dissent the refusknik had to present his or her alternative plan or strategy. Instead Havel explains dissidence as a kind of inner revolt which makes the dissident 'incapable of continuing to "live a lie"'. He argues that the dissident's motivation is existential first and foremost, and only in a secondary way, if at all, political. Indeed, the political motive behind dissent is the antithesis of Realpolitik, because it is actually a politics lying outside or beyond the sphere of power. According to Havel, however, dissidence does in fact effect change. But it does so mysteriously, in a 'hidden and complex way'.

> [It somehow] leads to something, summons something, produces some effect . . . even something as seemingly ephemeral as the truth spoken aloud, as an openly expressed concern for the humanity of humans, [and so it] bears within itself a certain power.

As we can see, Havel does not make big claims for dissidence. Indeed he underlines its obvious practical limitations, since it consists 'more in defending man against the pressures of the system than in imagining better systems'. If Higher Education could benefit more often from 'the truth [being] spoken aloud' as Havel puts it, that in itself would change things considerably. It would counter the lies, for one thing. And it might even help to make space in education for a less reductive ethos than the exclusively economic one that is currently predominant. The problem with this economic ethos is that it is too narrow; that it is based on 'gaming' and on 'rational choice'; and that it drowns out all sense of a more holistic, a more complex, a more irrational perhaps, but certainly a less reductive humanity.

Long before the fall of the Soviet Union, Vaclav Havel believed that East and West both had to rise to the same challenge, even if the political dilemmas they faced were different.

> [The] task is one of resisting vigilantly, thoughtfully and attentively, but at the same time with total dedication,

at every step and everywhere, the irrational momentum of anonymous, impersonal and inhuman power – the power of ideologies, systems, apparat, bureaucracy, artificial languages and political slogans. We must resist their complex and wholly alienating pressure, whether it takes the form of consumption, advertising, repression, technology or cliché – all of which are the blood brothers of fanaticism and the wellspring of totalitarian thought.

Havel's analysis of the way anonymised and depersonalised power works as a 'mere technology of rule and manipulation' is stark:

> Rulers and leaders were once personalities in their own right, with concrete human faces still in some sense personally responsible for their deeds, good and ill, whether they had been installed by dynastic tradition, by the will of the people, by a victorious battle or by intrigue. But they have been replaced in modern times by the manager, the bureaucrat, the apparatchik – a professional ruler, manipulator and expert in the techniques of management, manipulation and obfuscation, filling a depersonalised intersection of functional relations, a cog in the machinery of state caught up in a predetermined role.

As the fallout from the 'Arab Spring' of 2011 will confirm, if confirmation was necessary, it is easier to win the war than the peace, easier to topple dictators than to make the transition to a just democracy. It is also true that it is easier to attack individual figureheads (like Lawrence Summers or Alan Greenspan) than to confront the faceless bureaucracies, technocracies and kleptocracies so overwhelmingly pressuring democracy today. The relevance of Havel's description of power for Irish Higher Education is probably clear. When academic departments in Ireland moved, around the early nineties, and often at the instigation of their erstwhile 'heads-for-life', to rotating head-ships, this reform was not imposed from outside or from on high. The shift was experienced mostly as a liberation, all the more welcome in Ireland in that it followed a prior easing over several decades of the grip in which religious and political influences had pressured academic appointments and direction. So initially beneficial was the release from the concentration of power and authority in individual figureheads – whether druidic or secular, malign or benign, that few academics foresaw the oppressive nature of the bureaucratic machine that would eventually take over. Havel's answer to such mechanistic pressures is vigilant resistance: a deeply thoughtful, attentive and dedicated countering of deadening imposture.

HIGHER EDUCATION: LANGUAGE AND VIGILANCE

We have seen how, in today's world of Higher Education, words that have always enjoyed a positive connotation, words such as 'leadership' or 'freedom', are routinely emptied of their 'real' meaning. Certainly, the meaning of words is constantly evolving, but increasingly words such as 'community', 'conversation', or 'responsibility', let alone words such as 'quality' or 'leadership', can no longer be applied to Higher Education without completely denying their commonly understood meaning. And of course, if, as Humpty Dumpty tells *Alice in Wonderland*, 'words mean what I want them to mean', then we can do whatever we want with them, or indeed, behind them.

We have also seen that the problem with the fake or false language used to refer to Higher Education is not just the (cognitive) problem of inaccuracy. It is also the (moral) problem of dishonesty. Can the public see through the language of advertising and the language of propaganda currently surrounding the whole business of Higher Education? Possibly not. And yet the dishonesty and evasiveness of that language are arguably just as clear as in the infamously counter-productive example of verbal evasion supplied by the US counter-terrorist effort following

9/11: the expression 'extraordinary rendition' coined to refer to the unlawful abduction and detention of suspects ('ghost prisoners') in extra-territorial prisons ('black sites') for interrogation under outsourced torture. The unlawfulness of the operation was rinsed away by the neutral term 'extraordinary', just as the contractor's responsibility was diffused onto a host of (largely European) proxies, including transit stooges like Ireland.

In 1989 Vaclav Havel was reported in *The Independent* as declaring, 'I really do inhabit a system in which words are capable of shaking the entire structure of government, where words can prove mightier than ten military divisions'. *Academic Armageddon* is full of such words: the words of academic dissidents who have sought to protect the people working in academia 'against the pressures of the system'. It resounds with these dissidents' defence of the place of real thought, real language, and real humanity in Higher Education. Every single defence of what Havel calls the 'humanity of humans' chimes throughout space and time with the humane vigilance to which we are all called as human beings. No matter how little they 'count' politically, no matter how small the sacrifice made in order to make the defence audible. Such an echo sounded when a UCD professor of molecular pharmacology resigned his fellowship of the Royal College of Physicians of Ireland in protest against the failure of that body to take a clear and timely stand in the face of the victimisation of – Irish-trained – academics and medics by the Bahraini regime. With *Médecins sans frontières* (Doctors Across Borders) denouncing the spread in early 2012 to Syria of the practice that it calls 'medical warfare' (that is, the deliberate targeting of the injured and of the medics tending them), the resonance of the issue has been further amplified. All the more so since the same NGO simultaneously withdrew in February 2012 from its post-insurrection operations in so-called 'free Libyan' detention centres where its doctors were being used to patch up tortured detainees for further interrogation by the 'new democrats'. A similarly independent defence sounded when the Lord Mayor of Dublin confirmed in 2011 that he was opposed to the twinning of Ireland's capital city with the capital of a country whose regime imprisons and tortures political dissidents. Such protests against the ideology of 'profit *über alles*' are important verbal acts. They are worth highlighting here because they draw attention to the telling institutional silence within Irish Higher Education on the contradictions involved in doing educational business with un-elected, totalitarian or repressive (political) regimes. Certainly, their detractors will label such 'mere' words as futile, costing nothing and changing nothing. But words do matter. They can make a difference. When set against actions or inaction, words are what establish or negate credibility. And they are often most powerful when they expose silence or untruth.

At its most real, all education, including Higher Education, regards language watchfully. The foundation of all education is infinitely careful attention to what words mean and do. Perhaps there is nothing as demanding as trying to make sense of what somebody else says. Trying to weigh it up. Trying to tell what it really means. Trying to tell if it is true, or correct, or right. Trying to put it in context. Trying to work out what its real context is. To figure out if the person saying it believes it to be true or right. If that person is deluded or is being manipulated or is seeking to deceive or to manipulate. If their idea of what a certain word means is the same as mine or not. If the person speaking is being real, or not; is hiding behind a mask, a role or a function, or not. A whole life-time of education cannot take the challenge out of this effort to figure out what/whom we can/cannot trust.

Even if the marketing blather surrounding Higher Education today were not so repulsively false, the general linguistic climate is very challenging for educators. We are all flooded by the babble of constant, criss-crossing information flows, usually distort-ed into sound-bites. The omnipresent mediation and manipulation of words and images keep us locked inside a perpetual loop of stimulation. Our inner space is thus always pre-occupied. Digital technology is profoundly affecting the ways people communicate and interact, the ways that they multi-task, the ways that they manage distraction (emotional and cognitive, as well as digital) and the ways that they think, learn, imagine, dream, create and so on. We certainly need to understand more about these changes and about their challenges and potential. We need to be open to the palette of possibilities of new ways of being human, new ways of relating to each other and to the world and its diversity, possibilities and ways offered by all sorts of digital connections. Educationalists and educators in particular need to be open to the promise of other kinds of attention than the deep and slow solitary attention and endurance required to read a book carefully, in depth and in detail, from end to end. But even so, they surely need to remain true at some level, in some way, to the importance of thoughtfulness and attentiveness; they need to remain true to deep thinking, thinking unafraid of complexity or of contradictions. This may not suffice as a way of remaining true to the ideals of Higher Education, but without such vigilance or endurance we have no chance at all.

It would make a great difference if Higher Education could stem the flood of management-speak currently submerging the value and meaning of academic work. If that language could be changed, if students could re-envisage their studies as being about their own transformation rather than entirely about structures and processes, grades, 'points' and 'credits'. And if academics could communicate with college administrators about their students or about their teaching other than in electronic messages addressed to or signed 'Business Support'; and if they could enter their students' data in a system called something other than 'Business Objects', that would also be helpful. Of course, neither the problem nor the solution are merely linguistic. It would be wonderful if one wave of a warm word like 'community' could magic into being a sense of joint care of, and responsibility for, the university and all who sail in her. As it is, however, some of the administrations and figureheads most directly, if unmindfully, behind the most grievous and irreparable damage to the academic fabric of Ireland's Higher Education system can sweetly talk the talk of 'community', 'conversation' and 'responsibility'. The plausibility of this honeyed language of wholesome togetherness is belied, of course, by the facts. When the stampede to exit Irish academia into early retirement has been unprecedented, when the holdings of some university libraries are decimated and when libraries themselves are deserted, when students and staff who do not absolutely have to be on campus prefer to stay away, when (student) absenteeism and cheating have reached unprecedented levels, the gap between illusion and reality is uncomfortably stark.

If it is difficult to separate intellectual vigilance from linguistic watchfulness, it is also difficult to separate respect for language per se from respect for different languages or linguistic diversity. One of the most telling corporate reforms in recent Irish university history concerns the visual re-branding of the country's largest college, UCD. This expensively outsourced project issued in a new logo. The old 1911 coat of arms was not completely abandoned, but is now used only on 'ceremonial' or 'prestige' occasions. The logo presents a funkier design and a sharper palette than the crest. What is significant, though, is that, although the logo retains the harp (symbolising Ireland) and the three castles symbolising Dublin, it has been almost entirely stripped of verbal meaning. It features only one word indeed: the place-name Dublin, positioned below the acronym UCD. The idea behind 'Dublin squared', or the redundant doubling of Dublin in the pleonasm 'UCD Dublin', was to capitalise on the Dublin brand.

As UCD's more senior alumni will remember, the old crest had featured two mottos: one in Latin and the other *as Gaeilge*. The first, *Ad Astra*, means 'To the Stars', and it signaled the university's lofty, even stellar aspirations. Even more significant, if possible, the second jettisoned motto, '*Comhthrom Féinne*', meaning 'fair play', signaled the university's commitment to justice. Perhaps the point of the logo was to shake off continuity with an aspirational and idealistic past and indeed with language itself as a vector of continuity and meaning. Words and ideas (and even ideals) may still sell, but ideals expressed in Latin or Irish words were probably viewed as being well past their 'best by' date. However, it was not just idealism that was erased from the corporate logo and not just the languages of Ireland's scholarly past, Latin and Irish, but language per se, language as expression of memory, meaning and identity. And so the university that had once been home to wordsmiths of the stature of Gerald Manley Hopkins and James Joyce was left to face the world as a mute, wordless, pseudo-heraldic brandmark.

THE REPUBLIC OF WISDOM

As we have seen, Higher Education is not 'higher' because it promises higher levels of prestige, remuneration or power, but rather because it tries to focus human minds on higher and deeper levels of accuracy and truth, of attention and analysis, of understanding and openness and of complexity and uncertainty. Because of the huge range of areas and dimensions in which Higher Education seeks to develop this higher order thinking, it is probably too much to expect that all involved in it will always keep their eyes fixed on the prize. But this book suggests that, at the very least, Higher Education should not be subjected to any kind of structural, strategic or systemic manipulation which would necessarily militate against that aspiration. One of the golden rules that doctors are asked to follow, an essential part of the Hippocratic oath indeed, is to 'do no harm'. Those who seek to master-mind Higher Education should perhaps take the same oath.

Transcending all national and linguistic boundaries, all social and material barriers, the human republic of understanding must be open to all who are drawn to it. If the gate is locked, if the perimeter fence is too high, if the toll charged is exorbitant, and if those on the inside don't appear interested in thinking, then it's definitely not the right gateway: it must be the gate to something else. Perhaps it only opens inwards onto private property. Or onto the servitude of constant and perpetual measurement and competition. Higher Education is meant to offer an elevating avenue to a lifelong deepening and questioning of understanding. Ultimately it is meant to help us all to live well together.

Although Higher Education is traditionally the main avenue to that public good, it has not been the only one. Most Irish people have had the privilege of knowing deeply wise and thoughtful people who benefited from little, if any, formal Higher Education. That fact alone should make us all think hard about what institutions of Higher Education are for. And as for the institutions themselves, if they make of academic work a product to be sold for the highest price to the highest bidder, or if they denature the independent, searching spirit of students or teachers, they will soon find themselves marooned at best in an ocean of sham, at worst in the heart of darkness.

'Turning Darkness into Light'

The very expression 'Higher Education' is inherently aspirational. This book has dwelled on how its aspirations can be, and have been, suffocated. Although another would be necessary to suggest how they might be respected or resuscitated, it would have to start from the notion of truthfulness.

Living in truthfulness is never a matter of needing to 'be right'. Nor is it about wanting to have the last word. That is why this book will end by quoting a ninth-century poem written in Old Irish by a scholar-monk at work on the European continent.

The poem, *Pangur Bán*, was written in the margins of the manuscript that the scholar was copying. On his distant Dark Ages perch in the scriptorium, he portrays himself as blissfully engrossed in hunting down the word that will name 'what is'. Just as his white cat Pangur is fulfilling his feline nature by hunting mice at the monk's feet. For the scholar the hunt for truth is its own reward; it requires neither money nor fame, prestige nor power as recompense. I love this poem because it connects across the centuries with an anonymous Irish scribe who found an exquisite delight in a life devoted 'day and night' to 'turning darkness into light'. No doubt the tiny but timeless flame of his bliss will outlive the neon glare of our epoch's educational profiteering.

Pangur Bán

I and Pangur Bán, my cat
'Tis a like task we are at;
Hunting mice is his delight
Hunting words I sit all night.

Better far than praise of men
'Tis to sit with book and pen;
Pangur bears me no ill will,
He too plies his simple skill.

'Tis a merry thing to see
At our tasks how glad are we,
When at home we sit and find
Entertainment to our mind.

Oftentimes a mouse will stray
In the hero Pangur's way:
Oftentimes my keen thought set
Takes a meaning in its net.

'Gainst the wall he sets his eye
Full and fierce and sharp and sly;
'Gainst the wall of knowledge I
All my little wisdom try.

When a mouse darts from its den,
O how glad is Pangur then!
O what gladness do I prove
When I solve the doubts I love!

So in peace our tasks we ply,
Pangur Bán, my cat, and I;
In our arts we find our bliss,
I have mine and he has his.

Practice every day has made
Pangur perfect in his trade;
I get wisdom day and night
Turning darkness into light.

(Translated by Robin Flower)

Bibliography

Giorgio Agamben et al., *Démocratie: Dans quel état?* [*Democracy: The State It's in?*], La Fabrique, 2009

Kingsley Amis, *Lucky Jim*, Victor Gollancz, 1954

Stanley Aronowitz, *The Knowledge Factory: Dismantling the Corporate University and Creating True Higher Learning* , Beacon Press, 2000

Richard Arum and Josipa Roska, *Academically Adrift: Limited Learning on College Campuses,* University of Chicago Press, 2011

Michael Bailey and Des Freedman, eds., *The Assault on Universities: A Manifesto for Resistance*, Pluto, 2011

Stephen Ball, *The Education Debate: Policy and Politics in the Twenty-First Century.* Policy Press, 2008

Stephen Ball, *Global Education Inc.: New Policy Networks and the Neo-liberal Imaginary*, Routledge, 2012

Ulrich Beck, *What is Globalization?,* Polity Press, 2000 [*Was ist Globalisierung?*, 1997]

Thomas Benton (as William Pannapacker), 'A Perfect Storm in Undergraduate Education', Review of Arum and Roksa, *Academically Adrift*, in *The Chronicle of Higher Education*, 20 February 2011

Derek Bok, *Universities in the Marketplace: The Commercialization of Higher Education*, Princeton University Press, 2003

Marc Bousquet, *How the University Works: Higher Education and the Low-Wage Nation*, New York University Press, 2008

Samuel Bowles and Herbert Gintis, *Schooling in Capitalist America: Educational Reform and the Contradictions of Economic Life*, Basic Books, 1976

Pádraig A. Breatnach, 'Crisis in the Universities: The Impact on the Humanities', *Studies* 96:384, Winter 2007

Howard Brody, *Hooked: Ethics, the Medical Profession and the Pharmaceutical Industry*, Rowman and Littlefield, 2006

Roger Brown, *Higher Education and the Market*, Routledge, 2010

Paolo Coelho, *Like the Flowing River: Thoughts and Reflections*, Harper Collins UK, 2006.

J.M. Coetzee, *Diary of a Bad Year*, Viking, 2007

Stefan Collini, *What Are Universities For?*, Penguin, 2012

Mark Considine and Simon Marginson (eds.) *The Enterprise University: Power, Governance and Reinvention in Australia*, Cambridge University Press, 2000

Bronwyn Davis and Peter Bansel, 'Shaping the Hearts and Minds of Academic Workers' in *Journal of Curriculum Theorizing*, 23:2, 2010

Rosemary Deem, Sam Hillyard and Michael Reed (eds.), *Knowledge, Higher Education, and the New Managerialism*, Oxford University Press, 2007

Andrew Delbanco, *College: What It Was, Is, and Should Be*, Princeton University Press, 2012

Thomas Docherty, *For the University: Democracy and the Future*, Bloomsbury Academic, 2011

Frank Donoghue, *The Last Professors: The Corporate University and the Fate of the Humanities*, Fordham University Press, 2008

James Engell and Anthony Dangerfield, *Saving Education in the Age of Money*, University of Virginia Press, 2005

Bibliography

Francis Fukuyama, *Trust: The Social Virtues and the Creation of Prosperity*, Free Press, 1996

James Garland, *Saving Alma Mater: A Rescue Plan for America's Public Universities*, University of Chicago Press, 2009

Arran Gare, 'The Neo-Liberal Assault on Australian Universities and the Future of Democracy: the Philosophical Failure of a Nation', *Concrescence (The Australasian Journal of Process Thought)*, vol. 7, 2007

Benjamin Ginsberg, *The Fall of the Faculty: The All-Administrative University and Why it Matters*, Oxford University Press, 2011

Vaclav Havel, *Living in Truth*, Faber & Faber, 1986

Ellen Hazelkorn, *Rankings and the Reshaping of Higher Education: The Battle for World-Class Excellence*, Palgrave Macmillan, 2011

David Healy, *Pharmageddon*, University of California Press, 2012

Richard Hofstadter and C. De Witt Hardy, *The Development and Scope of Higher Education in the United States*, Columbia University Press, 1952

John Holmwood (ed.), *A Manifesto for the Public University*, Bloomsbury Academic, 2011

David Horowitz, *The Professors: The 101 Most Dangerous Academics in the US*, Regnery Publishing, 2006

Howard Jacobson, *The Finkler Question*, Bloomsbury 2008

Tony Judt, *Ill Fares the Land*, Penguin, 2011

— *The Memory Chalet*, Heinemann, 2010

Richard Keeling and Richard Hersh, *We're Losing Our Minds: Re-Thinking American Higher Education*, Palgrave Macmillan, 2011

Thomas Kelly (ed.) *What Price the University?*, National University of Ireland Maynooth Philosophical Papers, 2006

Rakesh Khurana, *From Higher Aims to Hired Hands: The Social Transformation of American Business Schools*, Princeton University Press, 2007

Annette Kolodny, *Failing the Future: A Dean Looks at Higher Education in the 21st Century*, Duke University Press, 1998

Walter Kirn, *Lost in the Meritocracy: The Undereducation of an Overachiever*, Doubleday Books, 2009

Robert Koukal, Review of F. Donoghue, *The Last Professors*, in *Technology and Culture*, Vol 51: 1, 2008

Anthony Kronman, *Education's End: Why Our Colleges and Universities Have Given Up on the Meaning of Life*, Caravan Books, 2007

Kathleen Lynch, 'Carelessness: A Hidden Doxa of Higher Education', in *Arts and Humanities in Higher Education*, 9:1, 2010

Alisdair MacIntyre, *God, Philosophy, Universities: A Selective History of the Catholic Philosophical Tradition*, Rowan and Littlefield, 2009

Czevlaw Milosz, *The Captive Mind*, Secker & Warburg, 1953

David Mowery, *Ivory Tower and Industrial Innovation: University-Industry Technology*, Oxford University Press, 2004

Cary Nelson and Stephen Watt, *Office Hours: Activism and Change in the Academy*, Routledge, 2004

— *Academic Keywords: A Devil's Dictionary for Higher Education*, Routledge, 1999

— *No University is an Island: Saving Academic Freedom*, New York University Press, 2011

Martha Nussbaum, *Not for Profit: Why Democracy Needs the Humanities*, Princeton University Press 2010

Patricia Palmer, 'Apples, Arts, Amnesiacs and Emigrants: The University Connection', *The Irish Review*, no. 8, 1990

Kate Pickett and Richard Wilkinson, *The Spirit Level: Why More Equal Societies Almost Always Do Better*, Allen Lane, 2009

Bill Readings, *The University in Ruins*, Harvard University Press, 1996

Gary Rhoades, *Managed Professionals: Unionised Faculty and Restructuring Academic Labor*, State University of New York Press, 1998

Bibliography

Henry Rosovky, *The University: An Owner's Manual*, Norton, 1991

Theodor Roszak, *The Making of a Counter-Culture: Reflections on the Technocratic Society and its Youthful Opposition* (with a new Introduction), University of California Press, 1995

Conrad Russell, *Academic Freedom*, Routledge, new edition, 1993

Ellen Schrecker, *The Lost Soul of Higher Education: Corporatization, the Assault on Academic Freedom and the End of the American University* , New York, The New Press, 2010

Malini Johar Schueller and Ashley Dawson (eds.), *Dangerous Professors: Academic Freedom and the National Security Campus*, University of Michigan Press, 2009

Elaine Showalter, *Faculty Towers*, Oxford University Press, 2005

Wesley Shumar, *College for Sale: A Critique of the Commodification of Higher Education*, Falmer Pres, 1997

Sheila Slaughter and Gary Rhoades, *Academic Capitalism and the New Economy: Markets, State, and Higher Education* , Johns Hopkins University Press, 2004

Gaye Tuchman, *Wannabe U: Inside the Corporate University*, University of Chicago Press, 2009

Brendan Walsh (ed.), *Degrees of Nonsense: The Demise of the University in Ireland*, Dublin: Glasnevin Publishing, 2012

Jennifer Washburn, *University, Inc.: The Corporate Corruption of Higher Education*, Basic Books, 2005

Alison Wolf, *Does Education Matter? Myths About Education and Economic Growth*, Penguin, 2002

Films

Up in the Air, 2009, directed by Jason Reitman

Heartbeat Detector, 2007, directed by Nicolas Klotz